REFLECTING
ON THE FUTURE
OF ACADEMIC AND PUBLIC LIBRARIES

REFLECTING ON THE FUTURE

OF ACADEMIC AND PUBLIC LIBRARIES

PETER HERNON AND JOSEPH R. MATTHEWS

An imprint of the American Library Association
Chicago | 2013

Printed in the United States of America
17 16 15 14 13   5 4 3 2 1

Extensive effort has gone into ensuring the reliability of the information in this book; however, the publisher makes no warranty, express or implied, with respect to the material contained herein.

ISBNs: 978-0-8389-1187-7 (paper); 978-0-8389-9601-0 (PDF); 978-0-8389-9602-7 (ePub); 978-0-8389-9603-4 (Kindle). For more information on digital formats, visit the ALA Store at alastore.ala.org and select eEditions.

Library of Congress Cataloging-in-Publication Data

Reflecting on the future of academic and public libraries / edited by Peter
    Hernon and Joseph R. Matthews.
      pages   cm
    Includes bibliographical references and index.
    ISBN 978-0-8389-1187-7
      1. Academic libraries—Forecasting. 2. Public libraries—Forecasting.
    3. Library planning. 4. Organizational change. I. Hernon, Peter.
    II. Matthews, Joseph R.
    Z675.U5R4435 2013
    027.473'0112—dc23   2012036382

Cover and text design by Kimberly Thornton in Charis SIL, Quicksand, and Gotham.

♾ This paper meets the requirements of ANSI/NISO Z39.48-1992 (Permanence of Paper).

CONTENTS

FIGURES, TABLES, AND TEXT BOXES

PREFACE

Many libraries face serious problems stemming from the economic recession of 2008–2009 and its aftermath, as well as from the ever-changing information-seeking behavior of their customers and the presence of information technologies that affect such behavior. In some instances, fiscal problems predate the recession. At the same time, there is an increased expectation that libraries demonstrate accountability, collaborate more with stakeholders and other libraries, and, in some instances, generate alternative sources of revenue. How should libraries respond to such pressures? Is it enough to continue to do the same things or, at most, introduce incremental change? On the contrary, we believe that the times call for dramatic transformational change and the creation of a vision of the future that excites library staff and stakeholders.

The mention of change management and the future of public, academic, or any other type of library suggests someone staring into a crystal ball and trying to predict the future. The emerging vision, as commonly portrayed in the literature on scenario development, might assume hypothetical facts and extend the projection for thirty to fifty years, but without producing anything relevant to help libraries anticipate, prepare for, and manage change. This book does not offer predictions; rather, it offers portrayals of the future through shorter-range scenarios, stories projected a maximum of fifteen years ahead. These scenarios contain elements or threads grounded in the present that libraries or other organizations can use as they piece together a story that is relevant to local circumstances and can be linked to strategic planning and change management. The goal is to help libraries produce a story that they can use to explore surprises and discontinuities in the planning process and to obtain staff and stakeholder buy-in to a vision that enables everyone to concentrate on the bigger picture.

The scenarios presented in chapters 5 and 8 do not represent an absolute vision; rather, readers can pick and choose among elements in different scenarios and add their own elements such as the ones presented in chapters 6 and 7. Chapter 9 suggests that scenarios also apply to the broader organization, and such scenarios merit review as library managerial leaders settle on the preferred future. The goals of this book are to identify relevant literature and possible scenarios and to get readers to think about the future and what the library infrastructure (staff, collections, technology, and facilities) will resemble.

We acknowledge that some useful scenarios have been offered for academic libraries, but our scenarios contain many elements not found in them. There is, moreover, a dearth of good scenarios for public libraries. Unlike other works, this one offers scenarios for both academic and public libraries at a time when many library managers may be consumed by the present and how to cope with scarce or reduced resources. We believe that the present serves as an opportunity to create a new and positive future, as some libraries are doing. After all, are there not dangers in thinking solely in terms of the present?

Reflecting on the Future of Academic and Public Libraries separates scenarios from scenario planning, and we believe that librarians can take any of the scenarios and apply scenario planning to explore a preferred future in more detail, factoring in local circumstances. We view scenarios as a tool for managerial leaders to use to generate discussion within the organization and with stakeholders as they prepare for a transformation that requires forming new partnerships, collaborating, staking out new service roles, and ensuring the workforce has the required skills, abilities, and knowledge to cope with change. As Joan Giesecke explains, "Libraries have a unique opportunity to begin to change how they interact with others in the higher education system because they are campus-wide entities that work with both the business and academic sides of the institution. Libraries can take a leadership role in bringing together different groups to explore possible partnerships."[1] Her comments could apply to public libraries and to the achievement of any transformational vision that requires relationship building to get others to accept, shape, and help to carry it out.

ALA Editions wanted a book that would alert those who are preparing to enter the professional workforce of academic and public libraries about how libraries are changing, what they might look like, and the types of skills they will need to prosper in the new setting. Through our many years of teaching in schools of library and information science, we have found that many of our students have impressions of library work that do not match reality or take into account the forces of dramatic change. Library directors may be flattening the organizational structure, merging and eliminating departments, starting new services, and participating more broadly within their communities. We cite key literature to reflect the changed environment, and the scenarios presented in chapters 5 and 8 have been reviewed by several influential library directors. Still, we recognize that no set of scenarios can be comprehensive; rather, they are suggestive.

We also see the audience of this book as comprising managerial leaders and staff of academic and public libraries as they move beyond the issues of the moment to piece together their vision of the library of the future. This audience extends to include the stakeholders with whom library managerial leaders deal, such as members of governing boards. None of these actors can afford to succumb to the idea that there is no longer any need for a library or that all resources are available on the Internet. Instead, they need to invest more extensively in advocacy as they stake out a future that can be realistically achieved—one that will take time to achieve—and as they convert library spaces to new service roles.

Reflecting on the Future of Academic and Public Libraries, our second collaboration, represents our many years of thinking about libraries and issues related to assessment and evaluation of library services. Through-out our careers we have witnessed many changes, some of which have been transformational. We have also observed dynamic leadership that propels libraries into the future and enables them to thrive in these times of uncertainty. We have invited some of these leaders to contribute their thoughts, as you see in chapters 6 and 8 and in appendixes A and B.

NOTE

1. Joan Giesecke, "The Value of Partnerships: Building New Partnerships for Success," *Journal of Library Administration* 52, no. 1 (2012): 36–52, http://dx.doi.org/10.1080/01930826.2012.629964.

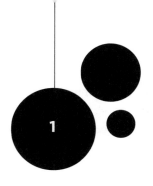

CHANGE—MAJOR TO MINOR

The purpose of the work on making the future is not to decide what should be done tomorrow, but what should be done today to have a tomorrow.

—*Peter Drucker*

The winds of change are blowing. Some of it can hardly be felt, but another part feels like hurricane force winds. The concept of change seems to be a bit of a cliché that can cause many people to yawn and say "so?" For others, the strength and variability of the winds may result in a reluctance to choose a new direction for their library. Linda S. Ackerman distinguishes among three types of change in an organization: *developmental, transitional,* and *transformational.* The first type may be either planned or emergent, but it is incremental and any change enhances or corrects existing aspects of an organization, often focusing on the improvement of a skill or process. The second type seeks to achieve a known desired state that differs from the existing one; it is episodic, planned, and perhaps radical. The final type, transformational change, is also radical, but it requires a shift in assumptions made by the organization and its members. Transformation can result in an organization that differs dramatically in terms of structure, processes, culture, and strategy. It may, therefore, result in the creation of an organization that continues to learn, adapt, and improve.[1] Much of the change in libraries historically has been developmental or, in some instances, transitional; however, with the economic recession that began in 2008 and its aftermath, there seem to be more instances of transformational change.

Naturally, the smaller the change, the easier it probably is to get staff to accept it. Transitional or transformational change is an emotional experience and might make staff worried or stressed—or, on the other hand, excited and optimistic. Developmental change might produce positive feelings. People tend automatically to scan a new situation for anything that is not to their benefit and then to complain about it. Such a negative focus often blocks their awareness of positive aspects, and they are unaware of, or resist, the direction the library's leadership wants to move the organization. Further, the organizational culture may be unwilling to change; the organization, in other words, may not be one that thrives on learning and change.

It is safe to say that the effects of transitional change and, especially, transformational change are profound and unpredictable for every organization, including libraries. To complicate matters, the rate of change is accelerating, particularly technologically. A library attempting to identify and understand the implications of every aspect of change faces a daunting task, and many miss some important ones. The result may be inertia and failure to distinguish among types of changes.

In reality, no one library is an island but rather part of a much larger, complex set of organizational relationships that exist within a community (academic or public entity) and the broader world of vendors, suppliers, and competitors. Further, new organizational relationships—partnerships and other forms of cooperation—are emerging as libraries cope with fiscal realities (see chapter 9).

Some libraries came into existence to provide the affordable sharing of hard-to-find, expensive, and unique books and other materials. The scarcity of materials and information allowed them to develop tools whereby they could control and organize access to the collection. In such an environment, the roles and responsibilities of the library are clear-cut and unambiguous. But libraries of all types no longer function in a world of information scarcity. They encounter the common perception among some stakeholders that everything is available via the Internet. For the vast majority of organizations, including libraries, the Internet has changed everything. In such an environment the roles and responsibilities of today's academic and public library differ from those of their predecessors, and similarly the roles and responsibilities of tomorrow's libraries will likely differ. The amount and speed of change signify that the foundation of the library is crumbling.

Fundamental Change

The foundations and physical structures of libraries, built over a long time, are undergoing dramatic changes. To think realistically about the future of libraries, we must challenge the assumptions, beliefs, and even worldview that dominated for many years. The order and structure of the information resources found in libraries were helpful to many people for more than a hundred years, but the information environment has changed radically and will likely continue to do so. As John Lombardi noted, "It is the physicality of the information medium that made possible the rationing, gate keeping, and in the case of for-profit scientific journals, profit gouging that are the key characteristics of the paper-based information age. With the dramatic decline in the cost of bandwidth . . . the threat to the monopoly of physical media grows exponentially."[2]

The Internet has brought chaos and a plethora of choices. To cope with this flood of information a new set of tools has been developed, ranging from search engines (e.g., Google), to sharing of information and other content (websites, blogs, podcasts, pictures, and videos), to building communities (Facebook), to purchasing goods and services (eBay and Amazon), to downloading of content (Apple iTunes), streaming and videos (Netflix), and apps for a myriad of purposes. Thomas Friedman, in a book about globalization and the contributing role of digital technologies, observed that "never before in the history of the planet have so many people—on their own—had the ability to find so much information about so many things and about so many other people."[3]

The Internet offers more opportunity for online collaboration, including carrying out scholarship that does not recognize geographic boundaries. Faculty and graduate students may depend on (and find more value in) an online community and not restrict themselves to the resources and services available from the local campus library. In some cases, faculty are less reliant on the physical library while becoming increasingly dependent on access to electronic journals and other digital materials, including digital archives.[4] Ironically, the library is becoming more "invisible" to the faculty, who often do not understand that the library licenses access to electronic resources on behalf of the faculty, staff, and students. In other words, many faculty and students fail to realize that the library provides the resources they cherish.

Many acknowledge that the media (audio, video, CDs, DVDs, books, e-books, streaming, and so on) through which they share information and knowledge will continue to change and thus the idea of a library as a collection of resources will endure. Yet others recognize the competitive environment in which libraries function and the role of the library as rapidly changing, whether the profession is willing to admit this reality. For example, Suzanne Thorin, Syracuse University dean of libraries, stated during the 2009 EDUCAUSE conference, "Let's face it: the library, as a place, is dead. Kaput. Finito. We need to move on to a new concept of what the academic library is."[5]

Thorin was prompted in part to make such a provocative statement by the popularity of Google, Wikipedia, and e-books; the reduced use of many academic library services; and the fact that many libraries are downsizing, condensing collections, and outsourcing many traditional services. Still, some academic libraries are evolving with the times and using the latest technologies to become centers of collaboration and communication.

One area of major change is the OPAC and its declining use in many academic libraries. Students may rely on databases and not search the catalog. As a result, is the OPAC becoming a librarian's tool, one that many users never think to consult? Further, students often prefer instant communication and skim for information rather than delve deeply into content.

Today, there are calls for repurposing libraries and creating spaces for dynamic and interactive learning. In many cases, librarians are relocating and reducing the size of print collections through off-site storage, use of automatic storage and retrieval systems, and digitization of portions of the collections. Such actions typically involve extended discussion with some faculty members who want to preserve "the good old days of being able to browse the collection." The migration from printed scholarly journals to licensed electronic publications continues, and, for some libraries, this transition has been completed. At the same time, some libraries are shifting reference desk service to circulation departments or are embedding librarians in academic departments to work directly and closely with faculty and graduate students. Anyone needing reference desk service consults the nonprofessional staff at a service desk or makes an appointment with a member of the professional staff.

Although not as important in public libraries, the preservation of information and knowledge remains an important role for many university libraries. Yet the economic reality suggests that preservation on a large scale is not an activity that every library can do on its own. Long-term preservation requires, for instance, moderation and control of temperature, moisture, and sunlight.

Jerry Campbell argues that, "because of the fundamental role that academic libraries have played in the past century, it is tremendously difficult to imagine a college or university without a library. Considering the extraordinary pace with which knowledge is moving to the Web, it is equally difficult to image what an academic library will be and do in another decade."[6]

Anthony Grafton has suggested that it is possible to divide libraries into two groups: old and new. On the one hand, "there is the traditional citadel of manuscript and print, closed and guarded, a hierarchical structure as neatly ordered as a vast set of display cabinets for butterflies. Its expert librarians pin every document, book, and journal in the collection to its proper place, the precise category equally expert researchers will be sure to find it." On the other, the "newer libraries are cast in a radically different formal language, one that speaks not of books, but of information: pellets of useable data, as smooth, precise, and indistinguishable as the *computer screens themselves*."[7]

Grafton also suggests that libraries face four crises at once:[8]

- A *financial crisis* caused by the proliferation of resources of all kinds
- A *spatial crisis* triggered by the massive production of print
- A *use crisis* caused by the transformation in scholars' working habits
- An *accessibility crisis* prompted by changes in the larger ecology of texts and reading

Some Important Trends

Obviously, libraries are transitioning from the traditional model of reading rooms and stacks of library shelving to areas that provide access to computers, social networking areas, places for quite study, coffee shops, and more. Thus, it is important to recognize trends that are likely to impact the academic or public library in the future. Here are some of the more important ones:

SOCIETY

Aging. The population is aging as the result of better health care, higher levels of education, and broader participation in the workforce.

Urbanization. The majority of the population live in or adjacent to large cities. As more people continue to migrate toward large cities, the split between rural and urban is likely to become more pronounced.

Households. Single-parent households continue to grow along with the number of people per household.

Demographics. The percentage of minority populations, in particular Hispanic populations, continues to grow, especially in the southern part of the United States.

Paper versus pixels. The downward trend in terms of the percentage of people who rely on newspapers and magazines continues as people spend more time online (with a variety of devices).

Generations. Young people have different values, expectations about life, and behaviors than their elders.

ECONOMY

Growth. The U.S. economy is in a period of stagnation or only slight growth as a result of the housing and Wall Street bubbles. For many, the "new normal" will be flat or declining funding for the library for some time to come.

Employment. The United States is facing a sustained period in which people lose their jobs or are asked to move to part-time or more casual work conditions. The prospect over the coming two or three years is not encouraging, no matter what political persuasion is discussing the issue. Given the globalization efforts over the past decade, the possibilities of higher employment are not encouraging.

Jobs. The world continues to move from a manufacturing and service economy to more of a knowledge-based economy in which there will be a constant demand for the right set of skills. This likely means that individuals will spend more time in formal and informal continuing education to ensure that their skills are timely and up-to-date.

Funding. The "new normal" public libraries are facing increased demand for their services but with reduced spending (as evidenced by reduced hours, closed library outlets, and a slimmer workforce).

CULTURE

Media. Traditional media sources are losing their influence as millions of people post their observations using wikis, blogs, tweets, pictures, and videos.

Risk aversion. Both in the society at large as well as in our libraries, we are less inclined to take risks.

Consumerism. The concept of an ownership culture is contradictory to the bedrock principles of librarianship, namely, free and shared access and the right to borrow material. There is increased interest in shared access and a competitive environment.

DIY. Do-it-yourself has become commonplace, so that people routinely remodel their bathroom or kitchen, build a deck, or scan items during checkout at the supermarket or library.

INFORMATION TECHNOLOGY

The Internet. The Internet has changed everything. Broadband access has reached almost 75 percent of U.S. households, wireless access is taken for granted by many people, and the apps for handheld devices are quite simply amazing with their creativity and usefulness. Web 2.0 is all about extending cooperation and collaboration around the world. The vast majority of people do their searching for information using a search engine (Google being the dominant choice).

E-books. Although the print version of the book remains quite popular, the rate of adoption and use of e-book readers is astonishing. During this past year, Amazon sold more e-books than print books. Some have suggested that we will soon reach a tipping point where e-books become the dominant form of published book. Others have suggested that the e-book is a major disruptive force, especially for public libraries (because publishers are reluctant to sell or license a copy of an e-book to a library).

Streaming. Streaming media, in particular videos and movies, will likely replace DVDs in the not too distant future. Streaming is responsible for more than half of all Internet traffic.

Mobile devices. Handheld devices such as the iPhone, Android phones, iPad, and Blackberry are becoming a daily necessity of life for a major proportion of the world's population. In addition, voice-over-Internet protocol (VOIP) is becoming increasingly common.

Cloud computing. Rather than host and maintain a series of computers (servers), any organization can now have its servers maintained at a remote site very inexpensively. In addition, rather than purchase a software application the library can now license the software (SaaS, Software as a Service).

Digitalization. Google Books has scanned some 15 million books, and more are being scanned every day. Other organizations are scanning books and making them accessible via the Web. The Google Book Search Settlement, whenever it is reached, will have interesting and profound implications for every library.

Speed of change. There have been fundamental changes in information technology: "From writing to the codex, 4,300 years; from the codex to movable type, 1,150 years; from movable type to the Internet, 524 years; from the Internet to search engines, nineteen years; from search engines to Google's algorithmic relevance ranking, seven years; and who knows what is just around the corner or coming out the pipeline."[9] Each of these changes has had a dramatic impact on the information landscape, and the acceleration seems unstoppable, making our attempts to understand and anticipate the consequences almost laughable.

Among the broad consequences of widespread access to the Internet are these:

- Information is no longer stored and retrieved (from a variety of places, including the local library) by people; rather, the Internet now manages information externally. This suggests a reduced need for local library collections. Eli Neiburger has suggested that "libraries are screwed" and that localness loses most of its value when anybody can retrieve something from anywhere in milliseconds. The value of the local copy is further diminished since there is little difference between transmission and duplication.[10] This means that collections are being disrupted as we move from atoms to bits.
- The Internet enables people to talk to and hear each other around the world with little effort (physical proximity to communicate in depth with a set of colleagues and friends is no longer a requirement). Collaboration can take place with people seemingly without the limitation of geography.
- There is an explosion of content creators in which people (lots of them) share photos, create content tags, contribute rankings and ratings, have websites, mix and remix digital content, are bloggers, use Twitter, and so forth.

- Libraries continue to underestimate the significant amount of information content being created online so that, rather than being islands of information, they are adrift in a sea of information.
- There is an explosion in the competitive market environment that is perhaps the most significant change facing libraries today.
- The challenge to remain focused is increasing as the Internet offers a plethora of opportunities for distraction (check e-mail frequently, read blogs, check out new videos on YouTube, pictures on Flickr). Connecting to the Internet allows us to work from anywhere while providing us with a set of tools to feed our seeming addiction for information about friends and colleagues, the joke of the day, celebrity news, links to interesting stories, pictures, videos, and so forth.

As libraries migrate from print-based collections to digitized resources, most of them find themselves in a confusing state called the *hybrid library*. There is increasing attention being paid to the provision of electronic information (access rather than ownership) with much less attention being paid to what to do with the paper-based portions of the collection. Reg Carr has suggested that the hybrid library is entering the "twilight zone."[11]

What is needed, according to David Lewis, dean of the Indiana University–Purdue University, Indianapolis University library, is for libraries to identify and "articulate their roles in the current and future information ecology. If we cannot or will not do this, our campuses will invest in other priorities and the library will slowly, but surely, atrophy and become a little used museum of books."[12]

In a call for dramatic action, Brad Eden, dean of library services at Valparaiso University, stated that libraries must take these steps:[13]

- Stop cataloging local copy.
- Acknowledge that the library's OPAC is not the place where individuals look for information—it is the last option or not even recognized as an option.
- Recognize that staffing levels are not likely to increase any time soon.
- Examine open-cloud solutions.
- Implement more cost-effective reference services.
- Move to a cooperative, shared integrated library system.

Some outside of the profession are joining the conversation about the future of the library. For example, Seth Godin made this argument:[14]

- The value of the library lies in its role of being the middlemen between the public and scarce content (books/information).
- The content of books and a vast array of other information are now abundant in the beginning of the digital era.
- People access information directly without the need for mediation by libraries and librarians.
- Therefore, libraries and librarians are no longer needed.
- To avoid extinction, libraries must transform themselves and move beyond the warehouse of content.

Not surprisingly, Godin's posting caused much discussion, within and outside of the profession.

Given the significant amount of change libraries are now confronting and will continue to encounter in the near future, they face two important questions: Where does their comparative advantage lie? How do they add value to the life of their customers? The goal for any stra-

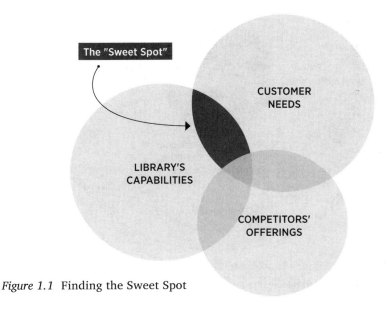

Figure 1.1 Finding the Sweet Spot

tegic planning process and use of scenarios is to find the competitive "sweet spot," as shown in figure 1.1. Librarians should review that spot in terms of both questions as they position themselves for competitive advantage, reconceptualize their community space, and maintain their focus on the information needs and expectations of customers. They show different roles for libraries and, in each instance, the focal point for libraries to concentrate on.

Creating the Library Compass

As we cover in the next chapter, change management focuses on a planning process and the plan, most likely a strategic plan, that emerges.

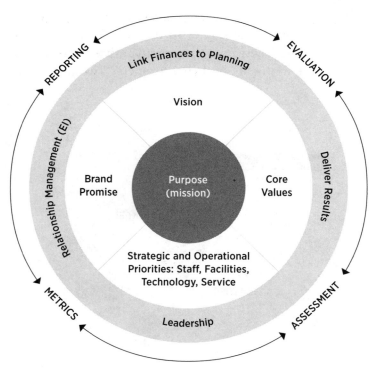

Figure 1.2 Generic Library Leadership Compass

Figure 1.3 Strategic Plan Compass

Reprinted with permission from Robert E. Dugan, University of West Florida Libraries, Office of the Dean of Libraries.

However, in today's environment there is an expectation that institutions will gather and report metrics of high interest to different stakeholders (e.g., a depiction of student retention rates, graduation rates, extent of user satisfaction, and cost of an education or the benefits students receive for their tuition dollars). Key questions are how libraries contribute to such metrics, and how they demonstrate that contribution to stakeholders.

In part, the answer might be the use of a *compass* that focuses on principles of excellence. For example, it might show the library as focusing, in part, on children and teens and fostering their "love of reading and skills in critical and creative thinking . . . from early literacy through mature readership—by offering a slate of services that provide academic support and intellectual growth."[15]

As Douglas A. Ready and Emily Truelove explain, some organizations, such as the Four Seasons hotel chain, have reconceptualized a compass, clarified its purpose, and repositioned the organization "for industry leadership." Their compass visually depicts "the organization's purpose, vision, core values (guiding principles), strategic and operational priorities, brand promise, and leadership behaviors or priorities."[16] Although not covered in the diagram, the organization should create metrics to reflect targets and milestones and to evaluate progress in achieving the organizational mission and vision. Those metrics should center on outputs (amount of use) and outcomes (tangible benefits from use of the library). Figure 1.2 adapts the compass Ready and Truelove lay out to fit libraries. Purpose is recast as the mission statement. Core values might relate to intellectual freedom and so forth, and brand promise explains what the organization stands for. Figure 1.3 recasts the generic compass to reflect how the dean of libraries at the University of West Florida views it as part of strategic planning linked to his organization and the institution as a whole.

An organization's elaborated compass includes the most important qualities, while some companion source, such as a web page link to the compass diagram, displays the full set of qualities. The targets and milestones for the university libraries, perhaps connected to such a page, would relate to sustained user satisfaction with resources and services and insights into student learning outcomes, institutional and organizational return-on-investment, collection strengths, and collaboration and partnerships with stakeholders.

In addition to placing the compass in a prominent place on the institutional website, it should also be included in planning documents, public presentations, and employee training manuals. The compass is a leadership tool around which to unite staff and stakeholders as the organization manages change and prepares for the future. It is therefore a figure that lays out where the organizational action plan will focus. Ready and Truelove refer to this as "collective ambition," since the elements in the diagram "help leaders spot areas of misalignment and launch initiatives to address them"[17]

Concluding Thoughts

Instead of merely focusing on maintaining the hours open to the public, creating a high volume of circulated materials and program attendance, a budget to support circulation, and extensive use of the building and digital resources, managerial leaders should think more broadly and develop learning organizations that look beyond the present. Leadership is often defined in terms of setting a vision and engaging the organization and its stakeholders in realization of that vision. Whatever change the organization engages in must be managed and viewed in the context of the mission, vision, and accomplishment of the strategic plan. The vision keeps the organization and its stakeholders focused on the aspiration set. Managerial leadership, therefore, considers both the present and the future. For this reason, it is important to keep the future in mind as the organization deals with the challenges of the present, perhaps, in part, related to issues connected with recovery from the global recession. As the library adjusts to the fiscal realities of the present, its managerial leaders must not abandon their vision of what the future library will look like in an increasingly digital environment and as scholarly communication and information-seeking behavior of many people continue to shift. Too much focus on the present will likely inhibit the ability of the library to prepare for the future and to connect with its stakeholders about a future, one that is perhaps vastly different from today.

Status quo thinking is a race to the bottom.
—John Bellina

NOTES

1. Linda S. Ackerman, "Development, Transition or Transformation: The Question of Change in Organizations," in *Organization Development Classics*, ed. Donald F. Van Eynde, Judith C. Hoy, and Dixie C. Van Eynde (San Francisco: Jossey-Bass, 1997), 45–58.

2. John Lombardi, "Academic Libraries in a Digital Age," *D-Lib Magazine* 6, no. 10 (October 2000), www.dlib.org/dlib/october00/lombardi/10 lombardi.html.

3. Thomas Friedman. *The World Is Flat: A Brief History of the Twenty-First Century* (New York: Farrar, Straus and Giroux, 2005), 64.

4. Ross Housewright and Roger Schonfeld, *Ithaka's 2006 Studies of Key Stakeholders in the Digital Transformation in Higher Education* (2008), www.serialssolutions.com/assets/attach_news/Ithaka-2006-Studies.pdf.

5. Steve Kolowich, "Bookless Libraries?" *Inside Higher Education*, November 6, 2009, www.insidehighered.com/news/2009/11/06/library/.

6. Jerry Campbell, "Changing a Cultural Icon: The Academic Library as a Virtual Destination," *EDUCAUSE Review* 41, no. 1 (January/February 2006), 30.

7. Anthony Grafton, "Apocalypse in the Stacks? The Research Library in the Age of Google," *Daedalus* 138, no. 1 (Winter 2009), 88.

8. Ibid., 97.

9. Robert Darnton, "The Library in the New Age," *New York Times Review of Books*, June 12, 2008, www.nybooks.com/articles/archives/2008/jun/12/the-library-in-the-new-age/.

10. Eli Neiburger, "Libraries at the Tipping Point: How eBooks Impact Libraries," a *Library Journal/School Library Journal* online summit, September 29, 2010; video, www.youtube.com/watch?v = KqAwj5ssU2c, and slides, www.slideshare.net/we2aam/ebooks-impact.

11. Reg Carr, "What Users Want: An Academic 'Hybrid' Library Perspective," *Ariande* 46, February 8, 2006, www.ariadne.ac.uk/issue46/carr/.

12. David Lewis, "A Model for Academic Libraries 2005 to 2025." Paper presented at Visions of Change conference, California State University at Sacramento, January 26, 2007, https://scholarworks.iupui.edu/bitstream/handle/1805/665/A%20Model%20Academic%20Libraries%20?sequence = 6.

13. Brad Eden, "The Status Quo Has Got to Go!" presentation at the Charleston Conference, November 8, 2011, www.slideshare.net/Charleston Conference/the-status-quo-has-got-to-go-by-brad-eden-dean-of-library-services-valparaiso-university-sat-930-am; video, www.katina.info/conference/video_2011_eden.php.

14. Seth Godin, "The Future of the Library," *Seth Godin's Blog*, May 16, 2011, sethgodin.typepad.com/seths_blog/2011/05/the-future-of-the-library.html.

15. Boston Public Library, "Strategic Planning: The BPL Compass: Principles," www.bpl.org/compass/principles/.

16. Douglas A. Ready and Emily Truelove, "The Power of Collective Ambition," *Harvard Business Review* 89, no. 12 (December 2011), 97.

17. Ibid.

BUILDING A PATH TO
THE FUTURE

*If we could spend just a fraction of the time and money we spend on trying
to predict the future instead on imagining preferred future options together,
we'd be living in a different world.*

—Edward Lindaman

Whether planning is called long-range planning, strategic planning, future visioning, preferred futuring, or whatever, the process of doing it is captured by some key questions: Where is the organization now? Where is it going? Where does it want to go? How does it get to where it wants to go?

In its most elementary form, to answer these questions planning consists of the following steps: monitoring, forecasting, goal setting, and implementation (figure 2.1). Monitoring, the first step and the focus of this chapter, is a process of identifying emerging issues in the external environment that pose potential threats or opportunities to the organization. This scanning activity, usually called environmental scanning or trend spotting, considers present and future factors that will influence the direction and goals of the organization. Planning, after all, is about the future and not just the present. OCLC, state and provincial libraries, coalitions of libraries, and individual libraries have all conducted environmental scanning.

Perhaps the oldest and most popular environmental scanning process uses SWOT analysis, which examines a library's strengths, weaknesses, opportunities, and threats (figure 2.2). Other organizations might apply similar techniques known as WOTS UP (weaknesses, opportunities, threats, and strengths underlying planning) or SOFT (strengths, opportunities, faults, and threats). Regardless of the name, environmental scanning enables libraries to assess current situations, outlooks, and prospects. Assessing the context of the current and likely future environment helps one determine what factors might affect the library. Having good information about the library's competition, knowing the library and its parent organization, and understanding the external environment are critical to performing a successful scan. As a library completes the scanning process,[1] it should address the following questions:

- What trends, government regulations, funding, and technology changes will likely affect the organization?
- Are the library's competitors known and well understood?
- How well is the library doing in the competitive environment? (Is use of the library and its myriad services increasing, decreasing, or staying about the same?)

Typically, a SWOT analysis, or one of its alternatives, starts with an inward, internal focus. The first task is to identify the library's strengths and weaknesses in relation to the marketplace. Each component of the analysis affects other components as well as the resulting vision for the future. To accomplish this task it is necessary to understand whom the library is and is not serving. A helpful exercise is to complete a market segment analysis (what segments of the community are or are not using the library?) and a service offering review (what services are or are not

Figure 2.1 Key Steps in the Planning Process

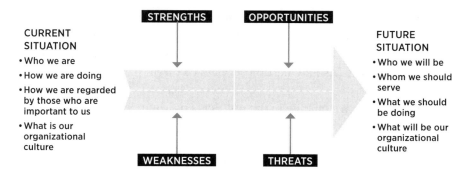

Figure 2.2 SWOT Analysis

being used). This exercise helps one identify unmet information needs of the customers and market segments that are important and not to be ignored. Among the tool chest of available methodologies, some libraries have used surveys and focus group interviews to understand the library and its services from the customer perspective.

One of the challenges of preparing a SWOT analysis is achieving a balanced and objective perspective. At times it is difficult to identify the strengths of the library and its services or to acknowledge limitations. Strengths and limitations might be associated with any aspect of the infrastructure (collections, services and programs, facilities, technology, and staff). Once the internal review has been completed, attention shifts externally. Here, too, it may be difficult to judge objectively what is happening without checking a variety of information resources and without using a technique such as TEMPLES (technology, economy, markets, politics, law, ethics, society),[2] SEPTEMBER, or the 5Ps (people, place, plant, process, and product [and service]). For illustrative purposes, here are sample TEMPLES questions:

Technology. What are important existing and emerging technologies and technology-based standards that might have an impact on the library and its ability to provide new or enhanced services?

Economy. What is happening with the economy, and would a downturn or expansion in the state or local economy affect the library's budget?

Markets. Has the ever-changing marketplace (for information resources and services provided by a library) created a new competitor or provided a new opportunity for the library? For example, are Internet-based reference services (Ask-a-Question services) a threat or a resource?

Politics. Is there a change in the political environment that might influence local, state, or national governments?

Law. Are there any federal, state, or local laws or other types of policies that might affect the local library? Changes in administrative law (rules and regulations) might also require a change in library service offerings.

Ethics. Are there clear policies regarding how the library acquires materials and services? For example, do all staff members adhere to copyright policies?

Society. Is society changing in ways that require a reexamination of the mission, goals, and vision of the library? Are the demographic characteristics of the library's customers changing?

SEPTEMBER covers the same areas, but "regulations" replaces "law" and "evaluation" becomes a new area.

One of the major hurdles associated with a SWOT analysis is that it often becomes nothing more than a brainstorming session to identify specific events and characteristics rather an exercise of critical thinking. The result is a list, often a long one, of things that may have direct or indirect effects on the library. A better approach is to consider each issue and identify the extent of its impact on the library. When adopting this approach, it is important to consider how each issue is phrased, develop priorities, and ensure that one issue does not conflict with another.

Once a prioritized list has been prepared, it should be shared with a broader audience consisting of the board of trustees, library staff members, stakeholders, funding decision makers, and interested members of the community. This audience evaluates each item and determines (a) whether the library's customers would agree that the statement clearly represents a strength, weakness, opportunity, or threat; and (b) what specific characteristic or aspect makes a particular factor or statement a strength, weakness, opportunity, or threat.

The SWOT analysis includes a clearly written description of the results. In some cases, a table summarizes the analysis and elaborates each statement and the factors covered in it. Typically, that summary of factors highlights the three to seven common themes that emerge. These themes are often referred to as *planning assumptions*. Perhaps the greatest shortcomings of a SWOT analysis are not looking far enough ahead and producing results that lead only to developmental changes to existing plans and strategies.

Environmental Scanning Reports

Environmental scanning has been described as "a kind of radar to scan the world systematically and signal the new, the unexpected, the major and the minor."[3] As such, it provides managers with useful information to engage in strategic planning by systematically gathering information external to the organization. The purposes are to lessen the randomness of information flowing into the organization; provide early warnings of changing external conditions as revealed from an analysis of trends, strengths, weaknesses, opportunities, and threats; and promote a future orientation in the thinking of management and staff.

Perhaps the best known of these reports is *The 2003 OCLC Environmental Scan*, which examined five landscapes to identify the issues and trends likely to impact OCLC and libraries:[4]

Social landscape. Three major trends characterize the information consumer who is comfortable in a virtual world: self-sufficiency (the individual operates in an autonomous way using search engines as gateways to both facts and answers); satisfaction (people are pleased with the results of their online activities; online access to information is easier, more convenient, and good enough relative to using the library); and seamlessness (the boundaries of work, play, and study are dissolving).

Economic landscape. As many countries face growing demands on centrally funded services, public funds for libraries will remain static or decline (remember, this was in 2003). Resources must be adjusted to emphasize an increasingly digital world, and libraries must demonstrate value.

Technology landscape. The pace of change is accelerating. Libraries should be investing in technology and standards to bring structure to unstructured and uncataloged data, and libraries should embrace open-source software.

Research and learning landscape. Three important trends are noted: e-learning is becoming more pervasive on college campuses; lifelong learning becomes a means for libraries to show how they add value; and the emergence of a variety of repository frameworks, metadata aggregation services, and richer content repurposing raises questions about what roles libraries should play.

Library landscape. The landscape covers four principal trends: as librarians retire, libraries often reallocate positions and create new job roles; funding agencies are increasingly demanding value; the library reacts to those who choose to visit it physically or virtually rather than being proactive and pushing content and services to the user; and libraries need to find more effective ways of collaborating with other organizations on campus and in the community.

Despite the call for action for libraries to consider different futures, this same OCLC report called for them to "reestablish our preeminence in search and retrieval, information and knowledge management, metadata creation and collaboration."[5] This was an unrealistic call for action; Google has dominated the search environment since the report was released. The OCLC report led to a plethora of other scanning reports in the academic library arena.

ACADEMIC LIBRARY ENVIRONMENTAL SCANNING REPORTS
Gregory Smith examined the issues surrounding the future of the library given the significant amount of change being experienced in higher

education.[6] He identified the most important issues facing an academic library as

- Displacement of paper by digital formats
- Primacy of the search engine
- Emergence of the digital lifestyle
- Changing patterns of scholarly communication
- Library as place

The New York University 21st Century Library Project resulted in a report, released in 2007, that incorporated a literature review and findings from an extensive set of focus group interviews.[7] The project team found that key trends related to technological innovation and consumer culture have a significant, but often invisible, impact on the expectations, comfort levels, and perceptions of library users. Among the major themes from the report are these:

Access to information is important. Users want convenient access to library physical and digital collections; expect expert and thoughtful cataloging of collections; may need assistance in navigating research resources; prefer tools that support serendipity in the discovery process; and recognize the need for long-term preservation.

Library as "gateway." The library should embrace tools and services that promote discovery and serendipity; encourage independence and idiosyncrasy; foster library transparency and seamlessness; and make it an active partner in the growing interconnectivity of social phenomena, academic scholarship, and technological innovation.

In 2008, the ACRL Research Committee prepared an environmental scanning report that listed the top ten assumptions for the future of academic libraries.[8] These assumptions, in rank order, are as follows:

1. There will be an increased emphasis on digitizing collections, preserving digital archives, and improving methods of data storage, retrieval, curation, and service.

2. The skill set for librarians will continue to evolve in response to the changing needs and expectations of the populations they serve, and the professional background of library staff will become increasingly diverse in support of expanded service programs and administrative needs.

3. Students and faculty will continue to demand increasing access to library resources and services, and to expect to find a rich digital library presence both in enterprise academic systems and as a feature of social computing.

4. Debates about intellectual property will become increasingly common in higher education, and resources and educational programming related to intellectual property management will become an important part of library service to the academic community.

5. The evolution of information technology will shape both the practice of scholarly inquiry and the daily routine of students and faculty, and demands for technology-related services and technology-rich user environments will continue to grow and will require additional funding.

6. Higher education will be increasingly viewed as a business, and calls for accountability and for quantitative measures of library contributions to the research, teaching, and service missions of the institution will shape library assessment programs and approaches to the allocation of institutional resources.

7. As part of the "business of higher education," students will increasingly view themselves as "customers" of the academic library and will demand high-quality facilities, resources, and services attuned to their needs and concerns.

8. Online learning will continue to expand as an option for students and faculty—both on campus and off—and libraries will gear resources and services for delivery to a distributed academic community.

9. Demands for free, public access to data collected and research completed as part of publicly funded research programs will continue to grow.

10. The protection of privacy and support for intellectual freedom will continue to be defining issues for academic libraries and librarians.

Rather than produce an environmental scan report, in 2008 the Council on Library and Information Resources hosted a symposium that focused on "reconceiving the research library." Several individuals prepared essays for reaction by symposium participants. As a result, some important issues are documented in the report *No Brief Candle*, which calls for aggressive action on the part of libraries in facilitating collaboration among librarians, faculty, and information technology experts; rethinking hiring practices by developing new career paths and opportunities for professional development; and eliminating redundancies as the library is reconceived to support better the goals of the college or university. Further, the report suggests that the twenty-first-century library should focus less on physical space and collections and more on organizing work according to the interests of stakeholders.[9]

In 2009, an ARL task force issued an environmental scan report that noted six trends pertaining to the library's role in research, teaching, and learning:[10]

- Profound shifts in research practices will push libraries to construct new forms of engagement and support.
- Research library collections and collecting have taken on new meanings.
- Research libraries will increasingly deploy services and resources into virtual environments inhabited by students, faculty, and researchers.
- Shifts in pedagogy to "active and engaged learning" are affecting how libraries partner with academic faculty to support student learning, scholarship, and productivity.
- Libraries will discover opportunities to engage nontypical students as we reinvigorate the definition of library.

- As university budgets tighten, many library building programs and new initiatives will face cutbacks and delays. There will be increased scrutiny and pressure to demonstrate return on investment. These pressures will incentivize some libraries to make profound organizational changes rather than incremental adjustments.

In 2010 the ACRL Research Planning and Review Committee prepared an environmental scan report that identifies these top trends affecting academic libraries:[11]

- Academic library collection growth is driven by patron demand and will include new resource types.
- Budget challenges will continue and libraries will evolve as a result.
- Changes in higher education will require that librarians possess diverse skill sets.
- Demands for accountability and assessment will increase.
- Digitization of unique library collections will increase and require a larger share of resources.
- Explosive growth of mobile devices and applications will drive new services.
- Increased collaboration will expand the role of the library within the institution and beyond.
- Libraries will continue to lead efforts to develop scholarly communication and intellectual property services.
- Technology will continue to change services and required skills.
- The definition of the library will change as physical space is repurposed and virtual space expands.

To the list of the top trends, we would add increased expectations that libraries engage in both evaluation and assessment research to improve services and to document the effectiveness of the library in meeting the institutional mission. By doing so, libraries focus on accountability, evidence-based planning, and decision making based on the evidence gathered.

As part of that environmental scan, ACRL identified the major issues affecting higher education that have an impact on "academic library budgets, clientele, and services, as well as librarians' relationships and roles within their institutions." The conclusion to this report notes:

While libraries are constantly changing, many of the issues mentioned in the ACRL environmental scan in 2008 are still recurring and examined in this document. Among them are the cost of higher education and its implications for libraries and information services; online education; increased accountability and role of librarians in assessment that will measure library experiences, information literacy and research skills, the advancement of technology, adoption rates and changes in Internet activity and behavior. While not exhaustive, the recurrent and emerging issues mentioned in this document will join the repertoire of significant issues facing the academic library in the near future.[12]

In 2011 the University Leadership Council commissioned an environmental scan to redefine the academic library.[13] The resulting report suggests that shifts of technology, changing user demands, and increasing budget pressures are forcing academic libraries to either adapt or risk obsolescence. Some of the important trends identified in the report are as follows:

Collection size is rapidly losing importance. Access is now more important than ownership.

Traditional library metrics fail to capture value to the academic mission. New measures of library success must emphasize the impact on student learning outcomes, retention and graduation rates, faculty research productivity, and teaching support.

Rising journal costs inspire calls for alternative publishing models. The steadily increasing cost of gaining access to electronic journals is unsustainable, and alternatives must be found.

Visible alternatives to the library now boast fastest growth and easiest access. The rise of Google, Amazon, and Wikipedia meet the information needs of the vast majority of individuals.

In 2010 the National Library of Scotland commissioned a report to identify the key influences on national libraries.[14] The report identified these as significant: changing patterns of publishing (e.g., the shift to digital publishing and electronic legal deposit); changing patterns of customer needs and behaviors; competition; political influences; and organizational change (workforce skills and leadership and agility). One of the recommendations, in particular, is of value to this book. That recommendation calls for an "agile library" that has a high return on investment, collaborates with external partners, and understands that its customers seek information in a competitive environment.

One interesting variation of an environmental scan are the provocative statements developed by a group of associate university librarians and associate directors who participate in the Taiga Forum. They agree with the ACRL Research Planning and Review Committee on some of the challenges, but their focus goes in other directions:[15]

- Flattening the organizational structure
- Engaging in "radical cooperation" among competing universities ("jointly-owned collections, deep outsourcing, shared staff, and shared services")
- Creating more partners for collaborative space planning
- Treating "books as décor" in redesigned facilities planning (for reading rooms)
- Engaging in on-demand purchase of books and other resources
- Viewing the library "in the cloud" (the delivery of digitization and Internet-based technologies as services rather than as products, dependent on campus collaboration).

Box 2.1, which summarizes the content of the environmental scans reviewed above, identifies a wide range of issues and forces that are affecting libraries today (and for the foreseeable future). It is important to understand the broader environment in which the library operates and to project from any relevant environmental scan which similarities and changes are likely in the future. Such knowledge may influence how libraries approach scenarios and select particular ones.

PUBLIC LIBRARY ENVIRONMENTAL SCANNING REPORTS

In England, a report suggested the importance of understanding social, cultural, and technological trends so that public libraries could be more

Box 2.1

Environmental Scans: Impacts for Academic Libraries

SOCIAL
- Self-sufficiency
- Satisficing—good enough is good enough
- Convenience
- Boundaries of work, play, and study are dissolving

ECONOMIC
- Funding will remain static or decline
- Shift to digital resources (with price hikes)
- Libraries must demonstrate value

INFORMATION TECHNOLOGY
- Pace of change is quickening
- Embrace standards and open source
- Displacement of paper
- Primacy of search engines (Google)
- Mobile—anywhere, anytime
- Digital lifestyle

LEARNING
- E-learning is becoming pervasive
- Repositories, metadata aggregation, richer content are raising questions about the role of libraries
- Changing patterns of scholarly communication
- Partner with faculty to support student learning

LIBRARIES
- Reallocate positions to nonlibrarians
- Demand evidence of value—traditional metrics do not do it
- Reactive rather than proactive
- Need to collaborate
- Redefine library as place, repurpose space, treat books as decor
- Access to information is important
- Rising journal costs necessitate alternatives
- Demand for traditional services is falling (fast)
- Physical and virtual space for contemplation and research
- Promote tools that aid discovery and serendipity
- Digitize more
- Assist in organizing work in the interests of stakeholders
- Move to patron-driven collections
- Collection size losing importance
- Organizational culture is stretched

relevant to community members.[16] The report concluded that ten drivers of change are especially worth noting. Among these were

Increasing mobility. People want to stay in contact with one another using e-mail or other online services.

Advancing technology. Changes and advances in technology are happening at faster rates. Handheld mobile devices are becoming even more popular.

Environmental sustainability. The library plays an important role in bridging the gap between the technological haves and have-nots in contemporary society.

About the same time, the Alberta Public Library Electronic Network commissioned an environmental scan that was prepared by KPMG, a well-known international consulting firm. That report identified six themes that deserved the attention of the library community, among them (a) public libraries are not on the political radar screen; (b) public libraries are faced with increasing costs; and (c) the changing role of public libraries.[17] Not surprisingly, if such a report were to be commissioned today, these same themes would likely emerge.

In 2006, Thomas Frey, a futurist, suggested that these ten trends would affect the future of the public library:[18]

Communication systems are continually changing the way people access information. Just a brief review of the past with various ways of communicating—telephone, radio, television, fax, e-mail, cell phones, Internet, podcasting, Facebook—will suggest that change is constantly present in this arena.

All information technology ends. All technologies used today will be replaced by something new. Media formats are constantly disappearing, replaced by something else. Something else will be more capable, faster, work better, and be smarter than what is available today.

The ultimate small particle for storage has yet to be reached. Moore's Law cannot be sustained indefinitely; the physical limits of data storage will someday be reached. And having a vast amount of data accessible online is a positive development, although the issues surrounding findability are much more important.

Search technology will become increasingly complicated. The next generation of search technology will move beyond text search and embrace image, audio, and video search.

Time compression is changing the lifestyle of library patrons. The world is speeding up, and the concept of "need" is also evolving and speeding up. People want information anytime, anywhere.

Over time we will be transitioning to a verbal society. Computers will become more human-like, with personality traits and other characteristics (no keyboards) that allow interactions with devices to be more verbal.

The demand for global information is growing exponentially. The ability to learn and understand the cultures of other countries will be fundamental as we move toward a global society.

The stage is being set for global systems. In addition to global systems we are already familiar with—trade, transportation, news services, time zones, stock trading, the Internet, and GPS—new global systems will be developed.

We are transitioning from a product-based economy to an experience-based economy. Library services need to move toward an experience that will be both interesting and fulfilling when someone visits the physical or virtual library. Books are moving from being a product to being an experience with e-book readers.

Libraries will transition from a center of information to a center of culture. The central role of the library as a repository of information is changing given the ready availability of information online. A culture-based library will be one that embraces the spirit of the community and is responsive to the needs of the community.

An environmental scan prepared for the Dundee Township (Illinois) Public Library in 2008 suggests that these, among other, societal trends influence library trends:[19]

Time compression. People are busier, and libraries need to save the time of the user (shades of one of Ranganathan's Laws).

Self-service society. People expect self-service, which also frees up staff to perform more important activities.

Reduction of privacy—by choice. People reveal much about themselves when they use such services as Facebook, YouTube, Flickr, and other social media sites.

Post-Google world. People are demanding immediacy and instant gratification. If a service is not available 24/7, then the service will not be used (or even thought of as an option).

In 2009 a group of Australian librarians and others gathered to develop a series of scenarios concerning the future of the public library (see chapter 4).[20] Among the major change influencers they identified are

Politics. The politics of identity, levels of government, infrastructure spending, personalization, the end of representative democracy

Culture. Popular culture, values, risk aversion, inward focus, consumerism, downshifting

Technology. The Internet, Web 2.0, e-books, other digital media, telecommunications, biotechnology, nanoscience, robotics, copyright

In 2010 the St. Paul (Minn.) Public Library embarked on a journey to develop a strategic plan. Part of that journey involved extended conversations and surveys of customers, citizens, stakeholders, and staff.[21] To guide the future of the library, some major themes emerged:

- The library should maintain its community/neighborhood focus.
- The library should explore ways to mobilize, to reach out into the community, offering site/neighborhood-specific materials and services.
- The library's website and digital services are important tools for the future.
- Partnerships and collaboration will be of utmost importance in the face of limited financial resources.
- A library is a place and more than a place. The place continues to be important to the community, and the importance of face-to-face interaction, with staff and with neighbors, must not be undervalued.

Finally, in 2011, an environmental scan report, prepared for the public libraries in the province of Ontario in Canada, identified external trends influencing library development:[22]

Literacy and education. Student literacy is being maintained or improved, one-third of adults have difficulty with simple reading tasks, home schooling is increasing, and distance (online) learning is becoming more popular.

Technology and telecommunications. Internet access determines how well one can function in society, 81 percent of households have Internet access, and broadband access for all has been established as a goal to achieve by 2015.

Consumer technology. Mobile technology is fast becoming a part of everyday life, location-based apps are popular, people enjoy and not merely consume products, social media is changing the way we communicate, and e-books have become the rage.

21st-century workplace. The workforce is getting older and people are working longer, collaborative teamwork is becoming the standard, information technology is embedded in almost all jobs, and the pace of change forces a culture of continuous innovation and enhancement.

Box 2.2 summarizes the results of the public library scans reviewed here. It indicates that the pace of change is accelerating, and that people are using new information technology to stay connected 24/7 (and, in the process, revealing much more about themselves).

The OCLC report *Libraries at Webscale* suggests that the Web has lifted barriers to how people communicate, conduct commerce, share data, conduct research, and create communities. The report calls on libraries to focus less on managing internal IT infrastructure and more on managing relationships, building partnerships, and creating value for the people they serve. Collaborating with other libraries (as well as with other organizations) will enable libraries to add functionality of interest for their customers.[23]

Thomas Frey suggested that there are true tectonic shifts taking place in the world of information and that seventeen basic forms of information are replacing books (and in the future that will likely be more).[24] Some of these book replacements are

Games. More than 135 million Americans play video games at least one hour per month.

Digital books. E-books outsold print books at Amazon in 2011, and about one-fourth of all self-published books are e-books.

Newspapers. Online readership of newspapers is up, and advertising revenues continue to plummet.

Photos. Every day more than 250 million photos are uploaded to Facebook (and many more to Flickr).

Videos. Netflix streams more than 2 billion videos per quarter, and Facebook users view more than 100,000 "years" of YouTube video each year.

Podcasts. Podcasts are becoming increasingly popular.

Environmental Scans: Impacts for Public Libraries

SOCIAL
- One-person households will increase
- Stay connected—online 24/7
- Demand for global information is increasing
- Environmental sustainability role model
- Moving to broader organizations (networks)
- Moving from products to experiences
- People lead busy lives
- People want personalized, customized service
- People are revealing more about themselves
- Population is aging, changing (immigrants)

ECONOMIC
- Static or declining budgets
- Need to demonstrate value

INFORMATION TECHNOLOGY
- Pace of change is increasing
- All technology ends
- Change in how people access information (and stay in touch)
- More and more data will be found online (in the cloud)
- E-books are the rage

LEARNING
- Demand for higher education will increase
- Lifelong learning is increasingly important
- Literacy at all ages is a continuing challenge

LIBRARIES
- Librarians are knowledge navigators
- Demonstrate value
- Disparity in range and quality of service provided
- Slow to change (getting out of touch)
- Need to become culture-based organizations

Apps. As of 2012, one in two mobile subscribers has a smartphone, and that figure is increasing steadily; in the past year, the average number of apps per smartphone jumped 28 percent.[25]

Courseware. In 2011, Apple's iTunesU had more than 500,000 available classes and 700 million downloads.

Personal networks. Use of social media, whether using Facebook, Twitter, LinkedIn, Google +, or Pinterest, is growing at a rapid rate. Facebook, for instance, has more than 1.1 billion subscribers and that number is likely to increase).

Concluding Thoughts

When reviewing the various environmental scans, libraries need to recognize that none of these lists are comprehensive and make judgment calls about which trends are important to them, factoring in local circumstances. Central to the use of these scans is the realization that, through scenarios, libraries stake out their vision of the future and the service directions they want to take. That vision guides the strategic planning process and goal setting. At the heart of this entire process is a judgment call. What to include or what to ignore as a trend influences how a group of librarians view the world as they create and review the library's vision, plan a new building, consider new services, or embrace a cooperative activity with other libraries.

In one striking example of a judgment call, the Arthur D. Little Company, an internationally recognized management consulting firm, failed to mention Google and the impact of its search engine in the "infosphere" of today when it submitted its environmental scan report to the OCLC board of trustees more than a decade ago.[26]

Thus, it is important to consider all of the trends identified in this chapter as well as additional ones. The future is too important to dismiss a trend casually, for it will likely be one with a significant impact in the future of your library.

The best thing about the future is that it comes only one day at a time.
—Abraham Lincoln

NOTES

1. Tim Hayward and Judith Preston, "Chaos Theory, Economics, and Information: The Implications for Strategic Decision-Making," *Journal of Information Science* 25 no. 3 (1999): 173–82.

2. Simon Wootton and Terry Horne, "*Strategic Thinking: A Step-by-Step Approach to Strategy* (Dover, NH: Kogan Page, 2000).

3. Arnold Brown and Edith Weiner, *Supermanaging: How to Harness Change for Personal and Organizational Success* (New York: Mentor, 1985), ix.

4. Adapted from OCLC, *The 2003 OCLC Environmental Scan: Pattern Recognition* (Dublin, OH: OCLC, 2003); to access the report, see www.oclc.org/reports/escan/. Reprinted with permission.

5. Ibid., 16.

6. Gregory Smith, "Academic Libraries in Transition: Current Trends, Future Prospects," *Christian Librarian* 49, no. 2 (2006): 101–108.

7. Cecily Marcus, Lucinda Covert-Vail, and Carol Mandel, *NYU 21st Century Library Project: Designing a Research Library of the Future for New York University* (New York: New York University Library, 2007), http://library.nyu.edu/about/KPLReport.pdf.

8. ACRL Research Committee, *Environmental Scan 2007* (Chicago: ACRL, January 2008), www.ala.org/acrl/sites/ala.org.acrl/files/content/publications/whitepapers/Environmental_Scan_2007%20FINAL.pdf.

9. Council on Library and Information Resources, *No Brief Candle: Reconceiving Research Libraries for the 21st Century*, CLIR Publication No. 142 (Washington, DC: CLIR, 2008).

10. Association of Research Libraries, *Transformation Times: An Environmental Scan Prepared for the ARL Strategic Plan Review Task Force* (Washington, DC: ARL, February 2009).

11. ACRL Research Planning and Review Committee, "2010 Top Ten Trends in Academic Libraries: A Review of the Current Literature," *College and Research Libraries News* 71, no. 6 (June 2011): 286–92. See also ACRL Research Planning and Review Committee, *Environmental Scan 2010* (Chicago: ACRL, June 2011), www.ala.org/ala/mgrps/divs/acrl/publications/whitepapers/EnvironmentalScan201.pdf.

12. ACRL Research Planning and Review Committee, *Environmental Scan 2010*, 2, 18.

13. Education Advisory Board, *Redefining the Academic Library: Managing the Migration to Digital Information Services* (Washington, DC: Education Advisory Board, 2011).

14. David Hunter and Karen Brown, *Thriving or Surviving? National Library of Scotland in 2030* (Edinburgh: National Library of Scotland, 2010), www.nls.uk/media/808985/future-national-libraries.pdf.

15. Taiga Forum, "2011 Provocative Statements," http://lisnews.org/taiga _forum_2011_provocative_statements. See also Local Government Group, "Change, Options, and How to Get There: Learning from the Future Libraries Programme Phase 1" (2011), www.local.gov.uk/c/document _library/get_file?uuid = c6349d6d-7b26-49e4-aee5-b476de21ecbb&group Id = 10171.

16. Ken Worpole, *21st Century Libraries: Changing Forms, Changing Futures* (London: Building Futures, 2004), http://cdigital.uv.mx/bitstream/ 123456789/6176/2/Doc.pdf.

17. KPMG, *Alberta Public Libraries Environmental Scan* (Edmonton, Alberta: KPMG, June 24, 2004).

18. Adapted from Thomas Frey, "The Future of Libraries," DaVinci Institute (November 2, 2006), www.davinciinstitute.com/papers/the-future-of -libraries/. Reprinted with permission.

19. Northern Illinois University, Regional Development Institute, *Environmental Scan Dundee Township Public Library* (DeKalb, IL: Northern Illinois University, 2008).

20. State Library of New South Wales, *The Bookends Scenarios: Alternative Futures for the Public Library Network in NSW in 2030* (Sydney, Australia: State Library of New South Wales, 2009), www.sl.nsw.gov.au/services/ public_libraries/publications/docs/bookendsscenarios.pdf.

21. Saint Paul Public Library, *Driving Forces Executive Summary: A Guide to the Future* (St. Paul, MN: Saint Paul Public Library, 2002), www.sppl.org/ sites/default/files/rcl/images/Management/driving_forces.pdf.

22. Frances Stocker, *Environmental Scan for Ontario Public Libraries* (Toronto: Southern Ontario Library Service, 2011), www.sols.org/links/ clearinghouse/strategicdev/resources/environmental_scan_2011.pdf.

23. OCLC, *Libraries at Webscale* (Dublin, OH: OCLC, 2012); to access this report, see www.oclc.org/us/en/reports/webscale/default.htm.

24. Thomas Frey, "Future Libraries and 17 Forms of Information Replacing Books," World Future Society (March 7, 2012), www.wfs.org/content/ future-libraries-and-17-forms-information-replacing-books.

25. "State of the Appnation: A Year of Change and Growth in U.S. Smartphones," Nielsonwire (2012), http://blog.nielsen.com/nielsenwire/ online_mobile/state-of-the-appnation-%E2%80%93-a-year-of-change -and-growth-in-u-s-smartphones/.

26. OCLC, *2003 OCLC Environmental Scan*, 1.

TRANSFORMING
THE FUTURE

Never be afraid to trust an unknown future.

—*Anonymous*

The process of creating a new strategic plan for a library is not rocket science; any group can create an effective plan. Creating a strategic plan does, however, require a fair amount of thought and effort. Strategic planning is a process whereby a wide variety of alternative strategies are explored for delivering library services. Figure 3.1 suggests a simple four-step process to produce that plan. Existing services are reviewed as part of the planning process to determine whether the service should continue. The number of services eliminated by any library during the planning process is likely to be few.

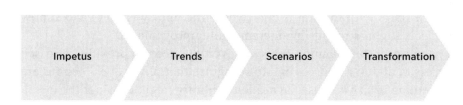

Impetus　Trends　Scenarios　Transformation

Figure 3.1 Strategic Planning Process

While the library engages in strategic planning, it should not forget the compass discussed in chapter 1, which can be used to link the planning process to the library's vision of the future as articulated in a preferred scenario. As this book indicates, the compass, strategic planning, scenarios, and scenario planning fit together and encourage everyone to think beyond the present and plan for the future.

Impetus

One of the challenges facing the planning process is to recognize the extent to which outside forces influence that process. As shown in table 3.1, the planning process can be either reactive—"muddling through"— or proactive. If a library responds primarily in a reactive manner, it does not really address the long-term needs of its customers; rather than focusing on the information needs and expectations of its customers, such a library is determining its own short-term needs. As a result, few changes occur. In contrast, a true strategic planning process focuses on the needs of its customers while acknowledging the impact of both internal and external forces directly on the lives of its customers and indirectly on the library itself. The result of a proactive approach to planning is that the library understands how it adds value to the life of its customers. One visible manifestation of such an approach is that a substantial amount of change takes place in the library over the next two to three years.

Most libraries go through a planning process on a regular basis (e.g., every three to four years). When considering thinking about and creating a new strategic plan, the challenge is to bring new perspectives and insights to the process. Many libraries, in fact, do not use the strategic planning process but rather engage only in minor operational planning, which starts with the status quo (where the library is now) and simply projects slight, straight-line incremental improvements.

As part of the planning process, given the need to provide increased access to digital resources and to recognize that physical collections are dwindling in size and use, an academic library might consider the installation of an automatic storage and retrieval system or participation in a regional (statewide) off-site storage facility. Reducing the amount of

Table 3.1
Forces Influencing the Planning Process

	REACTIVE	PROACTIVE
Internal to the library	Focus on immediate problems—increasing customer satisfaction, improving staff satisfaction	Focus on developing a more agile and responsive organization
External to the library	Focus on short-term performance issues—improving productivity	Focus on transforming the library to meet external threats and opportunities

materials housed in the library frees up space for other more strategically important activities.

Another example of a strategic planning process involves considering a range of alternatives and then selecting one that addresses specific customer concerns. Many of the individuals walking into a public library do not have a specific item or title in mind. Rather, they are likely to browse the collection in order to get a new DVD to view, get a do-it-yourself book to build a deck, and so forth. Yet the library has decided that its nonfiction collection must be organized in call number order following traditional library shelving protocol. Some libraries have explored strategic alternatives that promote browsing, including merchandising of its collection. Other libraries have abandoned the Dewey classification altogether in an attempt to be more customer-responsive, since they have found that a majority of their customers simply do not get that "Dewey thing."

Identifying Trends

To come to an informed understanding of the likely short-term future, it is important to have a good understanding of what is happening now. As noted in chapter 2, the best way to do this is to monitor or scan the environment (library, statewide, nationally, and globally) to identify the trends currently affecting or likely to affect the library.

The analysis and scanning activities need to be as thorough as possible in order to identify and measure the likely impact of each trend (huge, moderate, or minor). This gathering together of the trends allows the library to be in a position to create more meaningful (and likely) scenarios of what the future library is likely to look like.

There are several tools to help ensure that the scanning process covers all of the bases. A particularly useful one is PESTLE (political, social, technological, legal and environmental). Other approaches have different acronyms, including PEST, STEP, and SEPTED (socio-cultural, economy, politics, technology, ecology, and demographics). It is crucial to describe each trend and identify how and why it will affect the library. Once this has been done, it is useful to rate the potential influence. To accomplish this task, the library might involve a small group. A diverse team typically produces a better assessment of the trends and their likely impacts.

Strategic planning involves having an idea of what the future might look like. Types of futures might be categorized this way:

- Possible future—what *might* happen
- Plausible future—what *could* happen
- Probable future—what is *likely to* happen
- Preferred future—what you *want to* happen

Remember that surprises can profoundly affect a library. For example, prior to the announcement of the Google Books scanning project, the costs and time to complete the scanning of a large library collection were too high for any one library or for a group of libraries to absorb, and consequently the libraries could not offer digitized collections to their patrons. Google's decision to spend the large amount of money (clearly not large from Google's perspective) to create Google Books and make such digital collections available will have significant repercussions in almost every library (regardless of the eventual outcome of the Google Books settlement).

Building Scenarios

Although a library may find some of the scenarios or components of particular ones presented in chapters 5 and 8 to be of value for strategic planning, more likely it will use those scenarios as a basis for constructing its own preference. However, before settling on a particular scenario with all of its components, it is best to lay out possible futures to help managers think about how surprises and discontinuities can be examined in the planning process. Those futures might be told through stories or scenarios that build from those discussed in this book. The key is to construct different futures so that managers can assess alternative strategies that can be effective in a variety of circumstances. These stories are used to develop strategies that increase the chances of success for the organization as it responds to a changing environment.

Scenario planning, sometimes called scenario foresight, is not a process for predicting the future or developing preferred futures. Rather, the process asks participants to imagine multiple futures and then design plans to respond to changes depending on how the future develops. In essence, the organization can determine if it is headed in the right direction through the careful application of both scenarios and scenario planning.

Scenario planning involves the identification of the primary driving forces behind the trends discovered in the "Identifying Trends" stage of the process. Each driving force has an opposing force, so that the pair of forces forms an axis, horizontal or vertical, that can be used to create

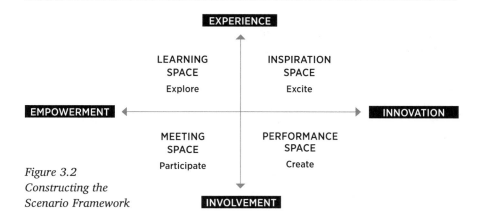

Figure 3.2
Constructing the
Scenario Framework

scenarios. A pair of axes is then selected so that it is possible to create four scenarios. For example, a library might choose the driving forces of *involvement* and *experience* for one axis and *innovation* and *empowerment* for the other, as shown in figure 3.2.

Combining the two terms adjacent to each quadrant, the library should then come up with an interesting name for each scenario in the framework.[1] In the example, the resulting four scenarios have been called the "Learning Space," "Inspiration Space," "Performance Space," and "Meeting Space." A single keyword is then selected to help communicate the essence of each of the four scenarios.

It is possible to expand the single keyword of explanation and provide more detailed information about the characteristics and implications for each of the scenarios. For example, table 3.2 identifies characteristics for the "Inspiration Space" scenario. When a library is developing a fuller list of the characteristics and their description for each of the scenarios, it is helpful to involve a wide range of people. Many find that a brainstorming or similar technique evokes a greater understanding and clarification of each scenario. Initially it is important to generate a large number of characteristics and, after a period of time, return and focus on editing the number to a more manageable set.

Once all the scenarios have been described and an associated list of characteristics developed, the planning group should identify the space implications, whether existing services need to be modified or eliminated, what new technologies (if any) are needed, what new staffing skills are required (for new hires or retraining), what workflow processes are needed, whether it is possible to partner with other organizations on campus or in the community, and so forth. If the group is large enough, it should break into four subgroups, and, by brainstorming, each should identify the implications of only one scenario. Once this has been accomplished, each subgroup should share its results with the whole group. Collectively, the group should generate even more ideas about the implications for each scenario.

Considering the case of the "Inspiration Space," it is possible to identify some key themes:

- Use of color, space, and design will affect people.
- Space should be flexible so that a wide variety of aesthetic experiences are possible.

Table 3.2

Sample Scenario Characteristics: "Inspiration Space"

CHARACTERISTICS	INSPIRATION SPACE
Value placed on space	Best use of space may change over time; space utilization important
Technology	Focuses on latest and greatest
Media formats	Digital/virtual
Information supply	Overwhelming
Work	Collaborative and digital
Space needs	Studios and theaters
Books	E-books
Family life	Delighting, surprising
Education	Just-in-time learning
Funding	Need to broaden source of funds, partnerships
Staffing	Techies, great people skills
Library services	Digital focus
Pricing	Free and user pays
Key user needs	Convenience, skilled assistance

- All types of media will be accessible.
- Visitors will be able to work independently or collaboratively using a variety of media types.
- Events will be staged that will surprise and delight the visitor.
- Guests will be able to customize the space without a great deal of permission or restraints being placed upon them.

Once a set of meaningful scenarios has been constructed, they should be reviewed by knowledgeable individuals who offer constructive criticism, and then it is time to move to the next stage.

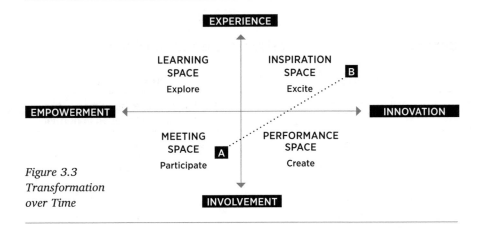

Figure 3.3
Transformation
over Time

Transformation

Once the library has decided to embrace and implement a particular scenario, it is important that it explore a variety of strategies to follow through. After the various strategies or strategy have been agreed to, the library must develop an operational plan that makes explicit the innovations, adaptations, and interventions needed to achieve the ultimate destination.

Naturally, the changes being planned will occur over time. Thus, as seen in figure 3.3, location A is where the library currently is and location B is where the library would like to be within the next two years. Thus, depending on the availability of funds, grants, partnership opportunities, and so forth, the library can begin to make changes and take incremental steps in the intended direction.

The process of transformation requires any organization to change. In reality, depending on the choice of the scenario and how rapidly the library, its customers, and other stakeholders would like to move, the amount of change may be quite significant. John Kotter has implored organizations to be much more agile and responsive to customer needs by embracing change projects with a greater sense of urgency.[2]

Successful transformation requires several different activity categories, as shown in figure 3.4 and is reviewed next.

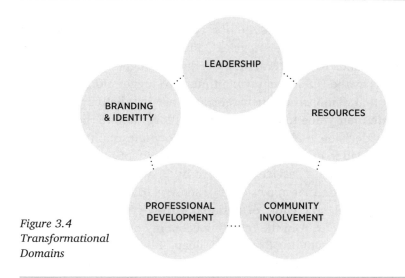

Figure 3.4
Transformational
Domains

LEADERSHIP

Every possible scenario for the future of the library presents challenges for the leadership of the library. The library management team obviously needs to communicate the chosen scenario and the reasons why the scenario best meets the needs of the campus or community. Involving the community in considering the various scenarios in a variety of settings—face-to-face community meetings, online meetings using blogs, Facebook and other tools—makes the resulting plan much stronger, since it is heavily shaped by the real customers of the library. The key is to remember that the role of an academic or public library remains important, regardless of how the library evolves to meet its mission better.

Library leaders must be responsive to the needs of their customers while helping them see into the murky future. Any leader listens to customers (using a variety of methods), tries to understand the winds of change that are blowing through the library, and shapes the organization to respond in ways that are dynamic and delightful to customers, stakeholders, and even staff.

FUNDING RESOURCES

Funding sources and their lack of diversity are at the heart of many library budget problems. Reliance on a single source for 90 percent or more of a library's funds makes the library dependent on the inevitable ups and downs of the financial cycles. Libraries must develop a more diverse set of funds to counteract the declining budgets of their parent organizations as the U.S. economy continues to stagger along.

Libraries that demonstrate their relevance are in a better position to communicate their value to the community at large and to their respective funding decision makers. Part of the economic reality for every library is the need to explore options for the delivery of services. Should it continue to provide X service supported by Y systems and staffed by Z people? One option that makes a lot of sense is to explore creating or expanding regional, statewide, or national library cooperatives so that the library can benefit from the resulting economy of scale.

Many observers, including Brad Eden, dean of library services at Valparaiso University, has categorically stated that the "status quo has got to go!"[3] He suggests eliminating many of the traditional library activities and being much more aggressive about creating winning partnerships with other libraries and other organizations.

COMMUNITY ENGAGEMENT

Every library, academic or public, needs to make connections with its customers, stakeholders, and the broader community. People are increasingly online and expect to be able to communicate with anyone, anytime. The library needs to ensure that it is where the people are, whether or not they are online. Many believe that public libraries need to become a local community and social networking hub as more and more resources become accessible online. Community engagement is also about developing and strengthening relationships with other organizations to produce a win-win situation for all concerned.

PROFESSIONAL DEVELOPMENT

Almost without exceptions, regardless of the scenario selected, libraries need to provide access to tools that enable customers to explore the possibilities of digital media and information resources. Customers visiting the physical library may want to "play around": learn new software, add new apps, and communicate with other customers and knowledgeable staff. The traditional approach of identifying a list of competencies and developing a set of classes to teach specific skills is much too slow in the digital world. Staff members need to invest in themselves and stay current with the latest set of tools and skills.

BRANDING AND IDENTITY

At the heart of every successful brand is the answer to this question: How do we add value in the life of the customer? Understanding how any library adds value is no longer as simple as it was in the days of restricted access to information resources (before the Internet).

Part of the branding process is recognizing the need to acknowledge the existence and power of competitors, such as Google, Amazon, and eBay. Opportunities abound in using social media such as Twitter, Flickr, and Facebook to engage customers actively when they are online. For a library to claim leadership in the information business is naïve given the plethora of evidence that people turn first to a search engine (and rarely to a library) when they need access to information. Still, there are significant opportunities for a library to create a brand that resonates with the community, so that even in these days of declining budgets it provides value in the life of its customers.

Concluding Thoughts

The process of using scenarios as a part of strategic planning is not overly complicated. Using the steps suggested in this chapter, a library can move in an organized, straightforward process to consider the impact of trends, develop likely scenarios, explore the implications of each of the scenarios, and then develop the strategies necessary to achieve the vision of the library.

> *If we have learned one thing from the history of invention and discovery,*
> *it is that, in the long run—and often in the short one—the most daring*
> *prophecies seem laughably conservative.*
> —*Arthur C. Clarke*

NOTES

1. Jens Thorhauge, "Transformation of the Public Library Concept in the Knowledge Society," presentation at the Library of the Future Conference,

Helsinki, Finland (October 13, 2011), www.bibliotekogmedier.dk/fileadmin/user_upload/dokumenter/om_os/Direktoeren/Taler_og_praesentationer/2011/The_library_of_the_future_Helsinki_october_13_2011.pdf.

2. John Kotter, *A Sense of Urgency* (Boston: Harvard Business School Press, 2008).

3. "The Status Quo Has Got to Go," full video presentation (60 min.), www.katina.info/conference/video_2011_eden.php; summary, www.theconferencecircuit.com/2011/11/06/the-status-quo-has-got-to-go/; slides available on SlideShare, www.slideshare.net/Charleston Conference/the-status-quo-has-got-to-go-by-brad-eden-dean-of-library-services-valparaiso-university-sat-930-am.

4

RELATED LITERATURE

Do not ask for answers to be given you. If given, they would not be yours and you could not live with them. Instead, live in the questions and little by little the answers will come. And you will live them also.

—*Rainer Maria Rilke*

As might be expected, the incorporation of new technologies and the Internet into libraries has had a profound effect on their infrastructure (collections, staff, technology, and facilities) and the provision of services. At the same time, there are changing patterns by which the public engages in information collection and use. With the economic recession and its lingering aftermath, dramatic change continues to take place in both academic and public libraries and the broader organizations they support. Those changes have sparked greater interest in the future and what libraries will resemble. Gone is the image of the twenty-first-century library as a Carnegie building, even one that has been renovated. Some envision a landscape without the existence of libraries (after all, is not everything available over the Internet?) or with libraries that are vastly restructured, perhaps maintained by the private sector. Others, of which we are included, see a long-term presence for the physical library housed in convenient, accessible locations but supported with numerous digital capabilities.

Such a library, as is widely recognized, does not represent the traditional view of a library as a warehouse for print collections (books and periodicals). The library provides access to numerous databases, some of which are global in nature. With book digitization, the availability of e-readers, and the circulation of digitized material, print collections are dramatically declining and, for public libraries, there might be a long list of people waiting their turn for digital copies of best sellers. One of the primary uses for public libraries today, it seems, is free Internet access, especially high-speed access.[1]

The purpose of this chapter is to draw attention to some key writings about the future of academic and public libraries. The criteria for the inclusion of these writings are that they advance future-oriented scenarios and challenge library managers and those to whom they report to reflect on various futures and perhaps to select the one that best meets the vision of those leading individual libraries into uncharted territory.

Scenario Planning

Nobody doubts that, as the second decade of the twenty-first century unfolds, librarians are trying to manage uncertainty, defined as the "unpredictable events in . . . [the] environment that [disturb] operations and performance of an enterprise." From an individual's perspective, uncertainty is the "inability to predict something accurately."[2]

Scenario planning—one way to explore, not forecast, the future and think about uncertainties—suggests futures that are plausible and challenge people's assumptions. The scenario-planning process recognizes that library managers can make choices that can lead down different paths. Those engaged in such planning construct various plots of what will happen during the transition from the present to the future state. With, for instance, the continued financial shocks since 2007, as the unemployment rate remains high and as cities and states continue to experience shortages in revenue, many libraries—academic as well as public—will continue to face funding crises similar to their parent institution or organization. Such a situation is not confined to the United States. Some public libraries, in Britain, for instance, face potential closure.[3] Aspects of different scenarios, especially those relating to collaboration, might have regional, national, or global implications.

Joseph Esposito, an expert on the publishing industry, has developed four scenarios for publishers that should be of interest to librarians engaged in scenario planning:[4]

Extensionism. A publisher has an existing business and wants to extend some aspect of that business into a new area. For many publishers, this is the default strategy. They are exploring options such as author-pays services, aggregation of content, and making content accessible on small mobile screens.

Face-down publishing paradigm. More people rely on mobile smartphones (and their small screen), no matter where they are. A handheld device is connected to the Internet cloud and can access a wide variety of services and content. It is necessary to have sophisticated and knowledgeable IT personnel, and it may also be necessary to partner with wireless phone companies.

Hybridization of online and physical worlds. Some companies, such as Apple, are doing an excellent job of reaching people on the Web, on the phone, and in stores. All marketing and service activities are designed to be integrated. Libraries can clearly do a better job of hybridization.

Library bypass. Publishers with existing library customers may be seeking to disintermediate their existing customer (the library) by reaching out to sell their product/service to the end user directly. If publishers think the library market is flat in terms of price increases, then this strategy may be very appealing. The challenge, of course, is that this will require direct marketing to individuals.

Box 4.1 lists some LIS writings on scenario planning; this book focuses more on general scenarios that library managers can review and alter to fit their vision of the future. From these scenarios, they might engage in scenario planning in order to encourage stakeholder and staff buy-in to the vision articulated. Clearly, scenarios enable the organization to keep its focus on the future despite momentary setbacks or problems.

Some Key Writings

Envisioning the future is not confined to research centered on the development and testing of scenarios. Perhaps the best-known discussions are Jerry D. Campbell's analysis of the academic library as "losing its supremacy" as the conveyor of "trustworthy, authoritative knowledge" due to "the impact of digital technology." Looking long-term, he asks, "Should the academic library be continued? If so, what will be its purpose? If serving as the world's primary source of trustworthy knowledge has in the past been the fundamental purpose around which libraries have evolved, what will be the fundamental purpose(s) around which libraries will continue to evolve?" He then concludes,

> Over the next decade, colleges and universities will have to make critically important practical and policy decisions about the function of libraries, about the space devoted to libraries, and about the roles of librarians. If these decisions are made wisely, the academy may be able to maintain much of the ineffable, inspirational value associated with academic libraries while retaining their practical value through altogether transformed activities and functions built upon a new mission designed for a more digital world.[5]

No Brief Candle, published by the Council on Library and Information Resources, identifies core functions and roles, challenges, and constraints for the academic library of the twenty-first century and offers a set of recommendations.[6] David W. Lewis sees the immediate challenge for research libraries as completing "the migration from print to electronic collections"; retiring "legacy print collections"; reconceptualizing the use of library space; repositioning "library, and information tools, resources, and expertise"; and migrating the "focus of collections from purchasing materials to curating content."[7]

"Promoting past success or defending status quo is a recipe for disaster." Sounding this theme, Elizabeth J. Wood, Rush Miller, and Amy

Some Writings on the Use of Scenario Planning in Libraries

Giesecke, Joan. *Scenario Planning for Libraries.* Chicago: American Library Association, 1998.

Hannabuss, Stuart. "Scenario Planning for Libraries." *Library Management* 22, no. 4/5 (2001): 168–76.

Hernon, Peter, ed. *Shaping the Future: Advancing the Understanding of Leadership.* Santa Barbara, CA: Libraries Unlimited, 2010, esp. chapters 10 and 11.

Kivilarvi, Hannu, Kalle Piirainen, and Markku Tuominen. "Sustaining Organizational Innovativeness: Advancing Knowledge Sharing during the Scenario Process." *International Journal of Knowledge Management* 6, no. 2 (April–June 2010): 22–39.

O'Connor, Steve, and Lai-chong Au. "Steering a Future through Scenarios: Into the Academic Library of the Future." *Journal of Academic Librarianship* 35, no. 1 (January 2009): 57–64.

O'Connor, Steve, and Peter Sidorko. *Imagine Your Library's Future: Scenario Planning for Libraries and Information Organizations.* Oxford: Chandos, 2010.

Walton, Graham. "Theory, Research, and Practice in Library Management 6: Managing Uncertainty through Scenario Planning." *Library Management* 30, no. 4/5 (2009): 334–41.

Watson, Richard. *Future Minds: How the Digital Age Is Changing Our Minds, Why This Matters and What We Can Do about It.* London: Nicholas Brealey, 2010.

Knapp want libraries to advance "traditional values while transforming operations and services." They also note that, if change continues at its present rate or accelerates, "it may be dangerous for libraries to become complacent."[8] Scenarios—those that do not argue for the status quo— become one way for librarians to envision alternative futures and manage their transition to the preferred one.

Transforming Research Libraries for the Global Knowledge Society focuses on libraries with institutional membership in the ARL and how they facilitate innovation and scholarly discovery as well as how they act as global centers for collaboration. The framework for their continued transformation is creation literacy, which involves the creation, dissemination, and preservation of new knowledge. Such literacy goes beyond information and visual literacy and "focuses on research output and its impact beyond the process of finding appropriate resources and solving problems for a given project or task." Furthermore, "creation literacy deals . . . with the knowledge and skills needed to choose a format and a venue for one's scholarship with high impact and access in mind."[9]

The final two scenarios highlighted in chapter 5 do, however, factor in embedded librarians who can partner with faculty in entire departments and disciplines by playing an active role in the teaching of information, visual, and creation literacy as well as the use and preservation of digital collections, and by engaging in data curation. In accordance with government and other funding agencies, libraries help researchers preserve data generated for funded research and partner with the teaching of the use of data archives—the collection of data sets generated from funded research.

Use of Scenarios in General

Instead of engaging fully in scenario planning, as already noted, it is possible to create and refine a set of scenarios or possible futures. Individual libraries can review the set, select one, or create a hybrid that includes content not limited to them. Such scenarios might focus on a particular area of library service or they might broadly provide a general overview of where the library is headed. Any of the narrower scenarios should be viewed in large part from the perspective of the entire organization and how this service advances the overall vision.

Nina W. Matheson used scenarios to illustrate the perceptions of directors of health science libraries about changes in the roles and functions of these libraries in the coming decade; neither of her scenarios (one highly desirable and the other highly probable), however, represent stories of the future as commonly associated with scenario planning.[10] Since then, Duane E. Webster has developed and refined a set of scenarios applicable to research libraries.[11] On the basis of those scenarios, it is possible to investigate a library's preference for a scenario and the staffing requirements. Larry Hardesty sees a challenge in attracting qualified professional staff to academic libraries. Many of them come to these libraries "in mid-life after examining and rejecting other opportunities."[12] Thus staffing becomes a key issue to accomplish any scenario and underscores the necessity of engaging in scenario planning—developing a plan to ensure that the staff of the future have the necessary skills, abilities, and talents; this is sometimes referred to as talent management. In effect, library managers engage in organizational readiness to accomplish the stated vision.

Peter Hernon and Laura Saunders developed a set of scenarios applicable to libraries at research universities and their participation in the federal depository library program.[13] Laura Saunders explores the preferences of academic library leaders for different scenarios about the future of information literacy,[14] and Maria Carpenter and colleagues use scenarios to examine libraries at research universities assuming different roles in scholarly communication: the open-access movement, data mining, publishing, and intellectual property.[15] Graeme Martin and colleagues present scenarios for the use of social technologies to involve staff in decision making and to enhance collaboration.[16]

Writings Relevant to Academic Libraries

Ithaka S + R (www.ithaka.org/ithaka-s-r), part of ITHAKA, a not-for-profit organization dedicated to helping the academic community use digital technologies, examines issues relevant to academic libraries, publishers, and scholarly societies, among others, to help them serve the changing information needs of faculty. Their findings, published in a series of reports, indicate a perceived decrease in the value of the university library by its constituent groups, contain elements useful in conceptualizing futures, and should be linked to strategic planning initiatives.

In one report, the authors identify a dilemma:

> If the library shapes its roles and activities based on what is currently most highly appreciated by faculty, it may lose a valuable opportunity to innovate and position itself as relevant in the future. On the other hand, if the library develops new

and innovative roles and services that address unmet needs, becoming newly relevant and even essential to those scholars who have moved farthest away from it, in the near term it may lose the support of its most ardent supporters. . . .

Can the academic library reengage with scientists? If not, is it realistic to expect humanists to remain wedded to it, given that humanists' declining support for the library's gateway role indicates they may be following in the footsteps of their peers in other disciplines, a trend which may only accelerate as a broader range of humanistic scholarly materials is made available in digital form? Addressing this dilemma is perhaps the most urgent strategic challenge facing academic library leaders.[17]

Writing in 2003 and drawing together several studies, James W. Marcum sees the driving forces for determining change in the academic library of 2012 as technological developments, library services, and librarians' roles.[18] A report from Denmark asks, "Is there a future for the research library? Which possible roles can the research library adopt? Can we draw a roadmap to help us move towards a new desired future?" The report then stresses that the future library will have to cope with changing information-seeking behavior of faculty and students; face a financial landscape that continues to be challenging, especially with the vast array of digital resources available; have a smaller workforce with different skill sets; and see a profession that questions its role in information provision and access.[19]

Daniel Greenstein, vice provost for academic planning and programs at the University of California, views the university library of the future as sparsely staffed, highly decentralized, and having a physical plant consisting largely of special collections and study areas. He sees outsourcing some library functions as the answer for institutions where budgets have been decimated by the economic downturn.[20] Additional insights for the development of scenarios come from Barbara Fister's interviews with more than 130 chief academic officers. For instance, she concludes that "librarians who do not produce will be reassigned or fired" and "the library will only house materials that are actively used."[21] John Dupuis's blog identifies twenty-nine reports on the future of academic libraries, including some not highlighted in this book.[22]

SETS OF MAJOR SCENARIOS

The University of New South Wales created three scenarios as it began the process of considering the future of the library and chose the "Learning Village," which supports learning experiences and a digital presence.[23] A working group of the Association of Academic Health Sciences Libraries developed five scenarios to assist its member libraries in developing strategic plans.[24] Rutgers University Libraries has developed four scenarios projecting different futures: more of the same, the digital library, virtual reality library, and personalized service library. For each, there is a list of attractive and unattractive features, a list of possible titles for each scenario, and some general reflections. The fourth scenario, for instance, which views "personalized service" as "synonymous with the Libraries," states:

> Each student and faculty member, upon entry to Rutgers, is provided with a personal librarian, who is available 24/7 by email, text, or other means. Librarians also make "office calls" or have designated space and hours within academic and administrative offices, dormitories, and dining halls. Webinars make distant interactions and collaborations available anytime, anyplace.
>
> Every morning, faculty, students, and staff wake up and are alerted to the latest scholarship matching their personal and professional interests, delivered to their preferred communication device. Any article or book of interest is easily downloaded or delivered to their door . . . [in their] . . . preference for viewing, marking and/or listening. Faculty and students can also easily "order" any book or journal directly from publishers and e-content providers.
>
> Primary source materials from the special collections of the Libraries have been digitized and are available anywhere, along with the customized "tools" to aid in scholarly discoveries. Librarians are also available to work with faculty and students to create personalized presentations, meaningful assignments, and teaching tools, all of which enhance classroom learning. Librarians will collaborate with faculty and students to manage, repurpose, and distribute their intellectual output.

>The Libraries website is no longer static, and members of the Rutgers University community have personalized portal pages that provide customized entry to information sources. Librarians provide instruction and assistance in optimizing the portals. The web presence extends deeply into other, non-Libraries hosted areas where users congregate virtually, such as Blackboard Vista and Agora. Required readings are automatically linked to course syllabi and students no longer have to purchase textbooks.[25]

These scenarios offer readers an opportunity to reflect on different service roles and the nature of future collections.

The library Scenario Planning Working Group of the Hong Kong Polytechnic University developed three scenarios to guide the strategic plan under development.[26] After engaging the university community and important stakeholders, the library leaders settled on the preferred scenario.

The ACRL sponsored the development of twenty-six possible scenarios that "represent themes relating to academic culture, demographics, distance education, funding, globalization, infrastructure/facilities, libraries, political climate, publishing industry, societal values, students/learning, and technology."[27] They identify which of these scenarios might most likely occur. The report authors raise four questions that anyone wanting to develop or choose a particular scenario should consider:

1. If this scenario were to exist today, would we be able to leverage it to our advantage? Do we have the resources, staffing, organizational processes, and strategy right now to take advantage of this scenario?

2. If this scenario were to exist today, in what ways are we currently vulnerable to the change it represents? In what ways are we unprepared, lacking in resources and staffing, or to what degree are our strategies and underlying values unable to respond effectively to the conditions this scenario represents?

Looking beyond current conditions, it is also useful as a strategic planning exercise to imagine proactively ways that an academic library could leverage this scenario in order to innovate. Strategic planners might ask:

3. Assuming we had all the staffing and resources we need (a very big assumption, we concede), what could we be doing to leverage this trend to our advantage?

4. What would need to happen—internally and in the external environment—for this vision to become a reality?[28]

In 2010, the ARL launched its scenario planning project, "Envisioning Research Library Futures: A Scenario Thinking Project," the purpose of which was to create a set of scenarios useful to member libraries in strategic planning and fostering organizational alignment around change. The four resulting scenarios do not lay out what libraries themselves will need to do to be relevant in the year 2030. Instead they describe the broader research environment in which the future users of libraries might operate. Within this context, librarians can imagine how academic librarians might fit into that environment.[29]

In 2001, the American Association of Law Libraries formed the Special Committee on the Future of Law Libraries in the Digital Age to explore the implications of electronic publishing on law libraries. The following year the association released sixteen scenarios grouped under three general headings: (a) "Creating Virtual Law Libraries in the Digital Age," which provides an overview of the virtual law library; (b) "External Collaborations and Expanding Staffing Roles in the Digital Age," which examines new roles for law libraries and librarians; and (c) "Establishing Repository Libraries and Library Consortia in the Digital Age," which focuses on shared collections.[30]

Writings Relevant to Public Libraries

In 2008 the State Library of New South Wales convened a committee to explore future scenarios. The Neville Freeman Agency conducted a study that produced four scenarios that place public libraries in the context of global developments. A two-by-two matrix of options was created from two broad dimensions: the impact of formation and communication technologies (chaotic to ordered), and libraries as space (physical to virtual). The resulting four scenarios were titled "Silent Spring," "How Buildings Learn," "Neuromancer," and "Fahrenheit 451."[31] Table 4.1 reprints the central characteristics for each of these scenarios. To envision the future of public libraries, in a different study, a team investigated the "professional skills and attitudes" that the staff will need in 2030 to carry out a given scenario and the leadership and funding necessary to achieve it. The team also identified twenty key influences essential to achieve each scenario (e.g., demand for space).[32]

Table 4.1

Characteristics of the New South Wales State Library Scenarios

SCENARIO NAME	1 SILENT SPRING	2 HOW BUILDINGS LEARN	3 NEURO-MANCER	4 FAHRENHEIT 451
Value placed on physical libraries	high and general	medium and niche	niche and high	niche
Impact of technology change	community	market-driven	anarchic	individualised
Key social dynamic	sustainability	innovation	anxiety	digitalisation
Society	survivalist	collaborative	bewildered	virtual
Economy	regulated	public/ private mix	open and chaotic	free markets
Technology	push-back	coveted	mayhem	saviour
Energy	energy efficiency	shift to re-newables	price spikes	clean tech breakthroughs
Environment	sustainability	technology solutions	resource shortages	sidelined
Government	local emphasis	smaller	ungovernable	e-gov/ politics 3.0
Information supply	controlled	co-created	overwhelming	managed
Information trust	trust in local	info savvy users	growing cynicism	smart filters

SCENARIO NAME	1 SILENT SPRING	2 HOW BUILDINGS LEARN	3 NEURO-MANCER	4 FAHRENHEIT 451
Work	localised	freelance/ contract	digital warriors	digital nomads
Space needs	focus on home	need for third spaces	safety/ comfort	telepresence
Books	honoured	equal status	niche player	e-platforms
Family life	extended	social networks	hectic households	fragmented
Leisure	rediscovered/ local	collaborative	online/ escapism	in short supply
Cities	green	reinvented	shift away from	racial tensions
Media formats	stable	more digital	total chaos	digital/ virtual
Education	protected/ traditional	lifelong learning	just-in-time learning	e-learning
Transport	public/local	smart transport	market pric-ing/chaotic	unnecessary
Social equity	cohesive	polarised	pluralistic	divided
Network	local focus	polarised	uncompetitive	virtual/global
Funding	low (gov)	high (private)	erratic (gov)	low (gov)
Copyright	open	in transition	unclear	closed
Staffing	low/ multi-skilled	low/specialist	status quo	automated/ virtual
Library services	stretched	extended	safe haven	digital focus
Library buildings	green	modernised	merged	virtual
Pricing	free	free and user pays	free	subscription and user pays
Library use	medium	high	low	low
Key library user needs	refuge/ local info	info facilitation	respite	convenience

Source: State Library of New South Wales, *The Bookends Scenarios: Alternative Futures for the Public Library Network in NSW in 2030* (2009), 22. Reprinted with permission.

A report on public libraries in New Zealand documents changes that occurred by the end of the twentieth century, and by doing so it produces a context for considerations of the unfolding new century.[33] A two-day seminar in Bedford (U.K.), organized by the Laser Foundation, offers observations about the future of public libraries and lists factors that affect that future (e.g., demographic population, social, and technological factors).[34] For the year 2015, "dynamic public library service . . . will need to build on its existing strengths" by emphasizing

- **Access:** virtual and physical access to services, wherever the customer may be
- **Support:** the information and support customers need to achieve their objectives
- **People-focus:** working out with customers what they need and then providing the services
- **Personalized service:** the services customers require, whatever their needs
- **Responsive service:** always listening to the customers
- **Dynamic service:** flexible, adaptable

The seminar report also offers a brief, general glimpse of the abilities and traits the professional staff will need, recommends Worpole's *21st Century Libraries* as "a useful starting point for a look at the library environment of the future," and discusses the library as a service organization rather than merely as a building.[35] Worpole suggested seven possible future scenarios for public libraries:

- The civic landmark
- The retail model
- The young people's library
- The neighborhood lifelong learning centre
- The themed library (joint venture)
- The mobile library
- The online library

Another excellent source from the United Kingdom is the Research Information Network website, which offers a series of reports and blog comments sponsored by the British Library and others.[36] These resources reflect the extent of a discussion about the existence of the library in the future and question the role of that library. One change will be greater collaboration than has existed before, and another will be tailoring services to the "Google generation" (those born since 1993), that is, adapting to how they search for information and what types of resources satisfy their quest for information resources.

A consulting company in the United Kingdom, Curtis + Cartwright, which is overseeing the Libraries of the Future site, has produced three different, but general, scenarios potentially applicable to the year 2050.[37] Two dimensions or axes were used to generate the scenarios—whether higher education has open or closed values, and whether the provision of higher education is dominated (funded) by the state or the market. The resulting three scenarios are cast in terms of societal values, such as the political, economic, technological, legal, publishing, and societal context; projections of the research environment; the role of teaching and learning; the skill set for librarians; and the role of librarians. These scenarios might be used to evaluate current strategies, develop new ones, engage in change management and planning, and avoid complacency.

In 2010 the British secretary for Culture, Media and Sport published a report on different visions for public libraries, which discusses five challenges for these libraries, among which are

- How can the library service respond to limited public resources and economic pressures?
- How can all libraries respond to a 24/7 culture and to changing expectations?
- How can the library service demonstrate to citizens, commentators, and politicians that they are still relevant and vital?[38]

One chapter of that report explores an additional question: How can the libraries upgrade the quality of their services—"to the level of the best?" In answering these six questions, the report lists core services, activities, and expectations (e.g., help for those using the Internet for the first time or searching for information). It also identifies activities and resources (e.g., free book loans, reference collections, study and job-hunting support, and public space).[39]

The Saint Paul (Minn.) Public Library has created "a framework for the future" that identifies driving forces, four scenarios that "paint different pictures of the future" for that library, and key trends; these stories complement this study.[40] There is mention of ten other models that offer very distinct services applicable to their communities:[41]

- The Houston Public Library, which delivers its services in a wide variety of ways, including a combination library and community center, express library outlets in various community and commercial sites, a "bookmobile" with computers, and a world language center.
- The Dibrary in Seoul, South Korea, which is a digital library, a giant computer laboratory that provides users computing facilities and access to an archive of digital material.
- Phone Booth Library in Westbury-sub-Mendip, England, which recycled its classic red phone booth into one of the country's smallest libraries, open 365 days a year, 24 hours a day.
- The Open Air Library in Magdeburg, Germany, which features books that can be borrowed any time of day from "cubbies" along the walls, a café, and a stage that hosts elementary school theater plays, public readings, concerts, and other cultural events.
- The Idea Stores, which are intended to rejuvenate the concept of the British public library. The Idea Stores in London take a retail approach to design and promotion and an expanded range of services and programming.
- Singapore's boutique or "life style" libraries are quite popular. The Library@Orchard caters to the needs of young adults ages eighteen to thirty-five. The Library@Esplanade serves as a one-stop resource library for the performing arts.
- Medellín, Colombia, which uses many strategies to promote learning and community building, including library parks, known as "hearts of knowledge," Park Book Stops, Traveling Boxes, and the Bibliocorner.
- The Human Library (http://humanlibrary.org), which is designed to promote social cohesion among people with different backgrounds, allows patrons to borrow a "living book"; a person volunteers to be a public representative of a particular group, usually a group about which stereotypes and prejudices exist.

- Biblioburro, in Colombia, which centers on the delivery of books and geography lessons to rural villages on two donkeys. Children also benefit from story times.
- Saint Paul (Minn.) Public Library, which during the 1940s and 1950s made books available at more than two hundred different points of distribution in the city.

The global economic recession, with its lingering aftermath, created opportunities for public libraries to demonstrate their usefulness to the community through higher usage statistics and engagement in meaningful outcomes metrics. Yet these metrics remain largely indirect, relying on respondent self-reporting, and have occasional vagueness in their wording.[42] Still, they suggest service roles that the community prizes.

Any discussion of the future must address the belief of individuals such as John D. Sutter, who maintains that "the stereotypical library is dying," the public library is "a community gathering place," and "books are being pushed aside for digital learning centers and gaming areas. 'Loud rooms' that promote public discourse and group projects are taking over the bookish quiet. Hipster staffers who blog, chat on Twitter and care little about the Dewey Decimal System are edging out old-school librarians."[43] Sutter notes other changes that merit inclusion in a discussion of the future:

- a multimedia space in the library "where kids shoot videos and record music"
- a blog dedicated to gaming and hosting video game tournaments regularly
- a space where children can tell stories and bring them "to life" through the library movie and music studio
- feed and text-messaging services
- staff monitoring of "local conversations on online social networks and using that information as inspiration for group discussions or programs at the real-world library"
- an "info column," where people share digital news stories
- an "info galleria," where patrons explore digital maps layered with factoids
- RFID-tagged book phones that kids point at specific books to hear a story.

Such changes mean that libraries are redefining the role, knowledge, abilities, and skill set of library staff. As Sutter reports, librarians are venturing "into the digital space, where their potential patrons exist, to show them why the physical library is still necessary."[44] Additional insights emerge from an examination of the assorted publications available from the School Book Library, which, among other things, views the public library as a community knowledge center and as a place known for its expanded use of information and communication technologies.[45]

Sven Nilsson sees future libraries as cultural institutions that focus on collections; collections remain "a focal point of the library" and serve as knowledge networks.[46] With all of the information available digitally and through the Internet, the challenges are to determine what to preserve and what to aggregate for individual use. To do so, libraries and others will have to repackage and tailor resources to meet customer expectations.

The OCLC report *Perceptions of Libraries and Information Resources* underscores the public view of libraries as places to borrow print books, but the public remains unaware of the assorted electronic content that libraries provide. In general, survey respondents are "satisfied with libraries and librarians, but most do not plan to increase their use of libraries." Furthermore,

> Respondents do indeed have strong attachments to the idea of the "Library" but clearly expressed dissatisfaction with the service experience of the libraries they use. Poor signage, inhospitable surroundings, unfriendly staff, lack of parking, dirt, cold, hard-to-use systems and inconvenient hours were mentioned many, many times by respondents. The overall message is clear: improve the physical experience of using libraries.[47]

Reporting the results of different surveys of the use of Danish public libraries, Niels Ole Pors finds that the public associates these libraries with books and discusses the role of these libraries as change agents. He notes that "more than 50 per cent of the users leave the public library in less than 15 minutes" and that people increasingly have digital resources and collections. "However, the data also indicate that it is pertinent to analyse the users in a segmented fashion as we do see many variations in relation to the different demographic background factors."[48]

American Libraries magazine notes that the employees of some future public libraries might be contract workers of for-profit companies.[49] In such cases, the companies might reduce services and make them more cost-efficient. Further, since 1981, Library Systems & Services, LLC (LSSI, www.lssi.com) has partnered with cities and towns to provide library outsourcing for new and existing libraries along with fulfilling contract library services for the U.S. government. As of 2011, LSSI was providing library management services across thirteen public library systems and sixty-three branch operations. Privatization is also seen in libraries in the United Kingdom.[50]

"Keeping Public Libraries Public: A Checklist for Communities Considering Privatization of Public Libraries," a report from ALA's Office for Library Advocacy, differentiates between outsourcing and privatization. In the former "the contract is typically narrow and for a specific service that can be easily defined and monitored," whereas the latter "encompasses all library services and controls not only how services are delivered but what services are offered and delivered."[51]

Kirstin Steele reflects on the concept of technological singularity, which maintains that artificial intelligence will someday surpass human intelligence, and expounds on the implications for libraries. She foresees a smaller workforce but the prevalence of "the traditional libraries . . . for decades to come." She thinks public libraries might become "like pawn shops or swap meets, where patrons pay admission or offer customer-made tinfoil hats and old books in exchange for data access." Her vision clearly differs from the older writings highlighted in this section.[52]

In summary, the various writings tend to refer to public libraries in terms of the physical building and access to digital resources. To maintain its relevance to the community, the library might be engaged in community building;[53] have extensive digital collections (e-books, e-audio books, and playaways), Kindles (or their equivalent), and laptops for loan, multimedia space for children, blogs dedicated to gaming, video game tournaments, info columns, and a gallery for sharing digital news stories and exploring digital maps; and be engaged in social networks. The library will be fully engaged with its community (per-

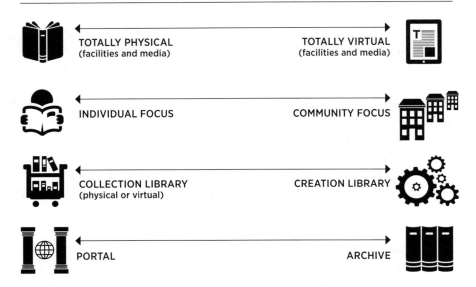

Figure 4.1 Alternative Visions for Public Libraries of the Future

The visions for public libraries of the future will consist of strategic choices along four distinct dimensions, each encompassing a continuum of possibilities lying between two extremes. Adapted from *Policy Brief No. 4* (Chicago: American Library Association, 2011).

haps encouraging the public to bring in photographs for scanning), complement traditional reference service with e-mail and instant messaging services, and offer assorted programs and services (e.g., healthcare screening, guidance for job interviews, and career services), but it will likely face cuts in funding and additional closings of branch libraries.

SETS OF MAJOR SCENARIOS

In the 1980s and again in the next decade, Bruce A. Shuman created a series of fictional scenarios to explore the future of public libraries. One of these scenarios focuses on the year 2022 and the library renamed the Cybrary. These scenarios are outdated and were never widely used.[54] In 2011, ALA's Office for Information Technology Policy published *Confronting the Future: Strategic Visions for the 21st Century Public Library*, which depicts different scenarios along four dimensions (figure 4.1).

Most public libraries, it is pointed out, "currently operate close to the physical end of . . . [the first dimension], almost all are being drawn toward the virtual endpoint by the rapid growth in the availability of digital media over the Internet. Where along this dimension will librar-ies aspire to operate in the future?"[55] In answering, libraries need not function at either end of a dimension. Different themes cut across and inform the four dimensions and associated strategic choices:[56]

Librarian competencies. Future librarians will become digital media mentors, fluent in the languages and structures of digi-tal documents and data and the availability of information re-sources on the Internet and elsewhere. As is the case today, they will need to have a good understanding of the users and the community they serve and their distinctive needs.

Collaboration and consolidation. A steady increase in various forms of collaboration and consolidation of collections will result from continued growth in the volume of library materials, both physical and digital; the shift in user demand from physical to digital materials; and financial pressures on libraries.

Digitization. The character of nearly all future libraries is likely to be increasingly digital. The hush of the stacks will be replaced by the whir of server racks; book checkout will become media download.

Personalization and social networking. Systems that enable libraries to supplement in-person recommendations with auto-matically generated ones will become increasingly available. Libraries also will use various social networking and messaging systems to reach out to their patrons routinely.

Archiving and cataloging. Libraries are likely to take on the archiving of locally important materials, both for local use and for access via the Internet and the Web. These materials may be community government records, personal memoirs, or his-torical items.

Pricing. One significant advantage libraries have over their com-mercial competitors is price; very few libraries charge their patrons for access to their materials and facilities, although they may limit such access to residents or users of associated libraries in other communities.

Concluding Thoughts

The literature on the future of libraries is a topic of great interest given the level of uncertainty the future holds.[57] Certain threads appear in the writings discussed in this chapter (table 4.2). It is clear that information technology will continue to influence the use of libraries and the information-seeking behavior of their users. Academic libraries have evolved from warehouses of stored books, and public libraries are now much more than lenders of books and DVDs. The services both types of libraries will offer illustrate that they provide more than books and reading matter. They seek a broad engagement with their communities. Such insights must be reflected in future scenarios as well as expectations from relevant stakeholders (see chapter 5). The scenarios proposed for research-intensive universities are less dependent on a workforce with degrees from accredited programs in library and information science. However missing from the discussions is the role of leadership to achieve a new vision and service roles.

The writings on the future of libraries, coming from librarians who are speaking to others in the profession, indicate the substantial questioning of the future library, be it academic, public, or other. There is need to engage a wider global community in the discussion of information-seeking behavior in the future and the place of libraries and other organizations in providing access to needed resources and technologies. Further, there is need to go beyond access to (and preservation of) information resources, as discussed in the following chapters, to identify the services in which libraries might expand.

Part of this broader communication might involve, for instance, the World Futures Studies Federation (http://www.wfsf.org), a global NGO founded in the 1960s to encourage and promote the development of futures studies among a cross-disciplinary, global community of "practicing futurists"—researchers, teachers, scholars, policy analysts, activists,

Table 4.2

The Future of Libraries: Common Threads from the Literature

SCENARIOS FOR ACADEMIC LIBRARIES	SCENARIOS FOR PUBLIC LIBRARIES
Changes to facilities based on faculty and student information-seeking patterns and expectations	Changes to facilities based on public's information-seeking patterns and expectations
Collaborative space sharing	Greater community role and serving the community in new ways
Elimination or consolidation of departments	Increased remote access to collections and services
New service roles for staff; staff reallocation and retraining; new skill sets and expertise	The library as more than the conveyor of books
On-demand purchasing of materials; combined collection development (e.g., jointly owned collections)	Staff with new skill sets and filling new service roles
Reconfigure services (application of technologies to continue the transformation of services)	
Take the library to the community	

and others from approximately sixty countries. They propose these collective goals:

- Investigate the future—study societal and future trends that have value across different service organizations.
- Offer different visions of the future—develop visioning workshops and futurist-focused seminars that involve more than librarians and that challenge long-held assumptions.
- Apply scenario planning—use scenario planning to explore, not predict, the future for individual libraries.

They are defending [the] library as warehouse as opposed to fighting for the future, which is librarian as producer, concierge, connector, teacher and impresario.
—*Seth Godin,* The Future of the Library

NOTES

1. For an excellent introduction to transformational changes, see *Redefining the Academic Library: Managing the Migration to Digital Information Services* (Washington, DC: Advisory Board Company, 2011), www.education advisoryboard.com/pdf/23634-EAB-Redefining-the-Academic-Library.pdf.

2. Graham Walton, "Theory, Research, and Practice in Library Management 6: Managing Uncertainty through Scenario Planning," *Library Management* 30, no. 4/5 (2009), 335.

3. Phil Bradley, "England's Libraries and the Funding Crisis," *American Libraries*, September 7, 2011, americanlibrariesmagazine.org/news/ 09072011/england-s-libraries-and-funding-crisis.

4. Joseph Esposito, "Predicting the Present," *Beyond the Book* (March 4, 2012), beyondthebookcast.com/predicting-the-present/.

5. Jerry D. Campbell, "Changing a Cultural Icon: The Academic Library as a Virtual Destination," *EDUCAUSE Review* 41, no. 1 (January/February 2006): 18, 22, 30.

6. *No Brief Candle: Reconceiving Research Libraries for the 21st Century* (Washington, DC: Council on Library and Information Resources, 2008).

7. David W. Lewis, "A Strategy for Academic Libraries in the First Quarter of the 21st Century," *College and Research Libraries* 68, no. 5 (September 2007): 418–34.

8. Elizabeth J. Wood, Rush Miller, and Amy Knapp, *Beyond Survival: Academic Libraries in Transition* (Westport, CT: Libraries Unlimited, 2007), xvii, xxii.

9. Barbara I. Dewey, ed., *Transforming Research Libraries for the Global Knowledge Society* (Oxford, UK: Chandos, 2010), 5.

10. Nina W. Matheson, "Perspectives of Academic Health Sciences Libraries in the 1980s: Indicators from a Delphi Study," *Bulletin of the Medical Library Association* 70, no. 1 (January 1982): 28–49.

11. Duane E. Webster, "Scenarios for Contemplating Research Library Futures" (unpublished manuscript, Simmons College, 2009); and "Organizational Projections for Envisioning Research Library Futures" (unpublished manuscript, Simmons College, 2010).

12. Larry Hardesty, "Future of Academic/Research Librarians: A Period of Transition—To What?" *portal: Libraries and the Academy* 2, no. 1 (January 2002), 94.

13. Peter Hernon and Laura Saunders, "The Federal Depository Library Program in 2023: One Perspective on the Transition to the Future," *College and Research Libraries* 70, no. 4 (July 2009): 351–70.

14. Laura Saunders, "The Future of Information Literacy in Academic Libraries: A Delphi Study," *portal: Libraries and the Academy* 9, no. 1 (January 2009): 99–114.

15. Maria Carpenter, Jolie Graybill, Jerome Offord Jr., and Mary Piorun, "Envisioning the Library's Role in Scholarly Communication in the Year 2025," *portal: Libraries and the Academy* 11, no. 2 (2011): 659–81.

16. Graeme Martin, Martin Reddington, Mary Beth Kneafsey, and Martyn Sloman, "Scenarios and Strategies for Web 2.0," *Education + Training* 51, no. 5/6 (2009): 370–80.

17. Roger C. Schonfeld and Ross Housewright, *Ithaka S+R Faculty Survey: Key Strategic Insights for Libraries, Publishers, and Societies* (New York: Ithaca S+R, 2010), 14.

18. James W. Marcum, "Visions: The Academic Library in 2012," *D-Magazine* 9, no. 5 (May 2003), www.dlib.org/dlib/may03/marcum/05marcum .html. See also P. Sennyey, Lyman Ross, and Caroline Mills, "Exploring the Future of Academic Libraries: A Definitional Approach," *Journal of Academic Librarianship* 35, no. 3 (May 2009): 252–59; Maria A. Jankowska and James W. Marcum, "Sustainable Challenge for Academic Libraries: Planning for the Future," *College and Research Libraries* 71, no. 2 (March 2010): 160–70; and Sue McKnight, *Envisioning Future Academic Library Services: Initiative, Ideas, and Challenges* (New York: Neal-Schuman, 2010).

19. Denmark's Electronic Research Library, *The Future of Research and the Research Library* (2009), accessed via www.bibliotekogmedier.dk/ fileadmin/publikationer/rapporter_oevrige/deff/the_future_research/ html/colophon.htm.

20. Daniel Greenstein, "Libraries of the Future," *Inside Higher Ed* (September 24, 2009), www.insidehighered.com/news/2009/09/24/libraries.

21. Barbara Fister, "Critical Assets: Academic Libraries, a View from the Administration Building," *Library Journal*, May 1, 2010, www.library journal.com/article/CA6726948.html.

22. John Dupuis, "Twenty-Nine Reports about the Future of Academic Libraries," *Confessions of a Science Librarian*, jdupuis.blogspot.com/ 2009/02/twenty-nine-reports-about-future-of.html.

23. Andrew Wells, "A Prototype Twenty-First Century University Library: A Case Study of Change at the University of New South Wales Library," *Library Management* 28, no. 8/9 (2007): 450–59.

24. Logan Ludwig, Joan Giesecke, and Linda Walton, "Scenario Planning: A Tool for Academic Health Sciences Libraries," *Health Information and Libraries Journal* 27 (2009) 28–36.

25. Rutgers University Libraries, *Scenarios for Contemplating the Future* (2011), www.libraries.rutgers.edu/rul/staff/planning/stratPlan11/Scenarios_for _Contemplating_the_Future.pdf. Reprinted with permission.

26. Steve O'Connor and Lai-chong Au, "Steering a Future through Scenarios: Into the Academic Library of the Future," *Journal of Academic Librarianship* 35, no. 1 (January 2009): 57–64.

27. David J. Staley and Kara Malenfant, *Future Thinking for Academic Librarians: Higher Education in 2025* (Chicago: American Library Association, Association of College and Research Libraries, 2010), 3, www.ala.org/ala/ mgrps/divs/acrl/issues/value/futures2025.pdf. See also David J. Staley, *Futures Thinking for Academic Librarians: Scenarios for the Future of the Book* (Chicago: Association of College and Research Libraries, 2012). For an excellent discussion of the use of these scenarios, see David J. Staley, Scott Seaman, and Eileen Theodore-Shusta, "Futuring, Scenario Planning, and Shared Awareness: An Ohio University Libraries Case Study," *Journal of Academic Librarianship* 38, no. 1 (January 2012): 1–5.

28. Staley and Malenfant, *Future Thinking for Academic Librarians*, 21–22.

29. Association of Research Libraries, "Envisioning Research Library Futures: A Scenario Thinking Project," www.arl.org/rtl/plan/scenarios/index .shtml. See also Charles B. Lowry and M. Sue Baughman, "We Do Not Know What the Future Will Be, except That There Will Be One," *portal: Libraries and the Academy* 11, no. 4 (2011): 887–94.

30. American Association of Law Libraries, "ARCHIVED: Future of Law Libraries in the Digital Age—Scenarios" (November 2001), www.aallnet .org/Archived/Leadership-Governance/committees/scenarios.html.

31. State Library of New South Wales, *The Bookends Scenarios: Alternative Futures for the Public Library Network in NSW in 2030* (2009), www.sl.nsw .gov.au/services/public_libraries/publications/docs/bookendsscenarios .pdf. See also Wells, "Prototype."

32. "The Future of Public Libraries" (n.d.), *What's Next: Top Trends*, http:// toptrends.nowandnext.com/?p = 603; also available at *Helene Blowers*, www.heleneblowers.info/2009/07/future-of-public-libraries.html.

33. National Library of New Zealand, *Public Libraries of New Zealand: A Strategic Framework, 2006–2016* (Wellington, 2006), http://kete .library.org.nz/documents/0000/0000/0036/StrategicFramework 2006.pdf.

34. Laser Foundation, "Libraries: A Vision. The Public Library Service in 2015" (Lancashire, UK, 2011), 5.

35. Ibid., 13, 20. See also Ken Worpole, *21st Century Libraries: Changing Form, Changing Futures* (Building Futures, 2004), www.cabe.org.uk/ files/21st-century-libraries.pdf.

36. Research Information Network, www.researchinfonet.org/libraries/.

37. Curtis + Cartwright, *Academic Libraries of the Future: Scenarios for 2050* (Surrey, UK: Curtis + Cartwright Consulting, 2011). For a synopsis of those scenarios, see www.futurelibraries.info/content/page/scenarios-2050-0.

38. The Secretary of State for Culture, Media and Sport, *The Modernisation Review of Public Libraries: A Policy Statement* (London: Stationery Office, 2010), 3.

39. Ibid., 52–53.

40. *Saint Paul Public Library: A Framework for the Future* (St. Paul, MN: Saint Paul Public Library, 2010), 1, www.sppl.org/sites/default/files/rcl/images/Management/stories.pdf.

41. Saint Paul Public Library, *Driving Forces Executive Summary: A Guide to the Future*, prepared by Beldon Charles (St. Paul, MN: Saint Paul Public Library, 2010), 23–24, www.sppl.org/sites/default/files/rcl/images/management/driving_forces.pdf. Reprinted with permission.

42. See Samantha Becker, Michael D. Crandall, Karen E. Fisher, Bo Kinney, Carol Landry, and Anita Rocha, *Opportunity for All: How the American Public Benefits from Internet Access at U.S. Libraries* (Washington, DC: Institute of Museum and Library Services, 2010), http://tascha.washington.edu/usimpact.

43. John D. Sutter, "The Future of Libraries, with or without Books," *CNN.com/Technology* (September 3, 2009), www.cnn.com/2009/TECH/09/04/future.library.technology/.

44. Ibid.

45. World Public Library, *Public Libraries International Network Collection*, http://worldlibrary.net/Collection.aspx?collection=74.

46. Sven Nilsson, "A Future Scenario: A Library for All Times" (n.d.), www.futurum.polyvalent.se/future.htm. See also A Space for the Future-Library Buildings in the 21st Century, a conference organized by Helsinki City Library and Hanasaari Cultural Centre, June 2–3, 2002, Finland, http://pandora.lib.hel.fi/conf02/.

47. OCLC, *Perceptions of Libraries and Information Resources* (Dublin, OH: OCLC Online Computer Library Center, Inc., 2005), 6–6, www.oclc.org/reports/pdfs/Percept_all.pdf.

48. Niels Ole Pors, "Burning Platforms and Melting Icebergs: An Exploratory Analysis of Present Strategic Challenges and Cross-Pressures in the Public Libraries," *Performance Measurement and Metrics* 11, no. 1 (2010), 22.

49. Beverly Goldberg, "California Groups Oppose Library Privatization Talks," *American Libraries*, July 14, 2010, http://americanlibrariesmagazine.org/news/07142010/california-groups-oppose-library-privatization-talks.

50. Beverly Goldberg, "Privatization, and Pushback, Proceed in U.S., U.K.," *American Libraries* 42, no. 7/8 (July/August 2011): 15.

51. Ibid., 16. See also American Library Association, Office for Library Advocacy, "Keeping Public Libraries Public: A Checklist for Communities Considering Privatization of Public Libraries," www.ala.org/tools/sites/

ala.org.tools/files/content/outsourcing/REVISEDSEPT2011_ALAKeeping PublicLibraries%20PublicFINAL2.pdf.

52. Kirstin Steele, "The Singularity and the Library," *The Bottom Line: Managing Library Finances* 24, no. 4 (2011), 229.

53. Urban Libraries Council, *The Engaged Library: Chicago Stories of Community Building* (Chicago: Urban Libraries Council, n.d.), http://urbanlibraries .org/associations/9851/files/ULC_PFSC_Engaged_0206.pdf. "Relevancy of Libraries in the Future," *LISNews*, May 22, 2009, lisnews.org/relevancy _libraries_future, reinforces the topic of relevance. See also *America's Digital Future: Advancing a Shared Strategy for Digital Public Libraries* (Dublin, OH: OCLC, 2012, www.oclc.org/content/dam/campaign-land-ing-pages/en/ndpl-report.pdf.

54. Bruce A. Shuman, *Beyond the Library of the Future: Alternative Futures for the Public Library* (Englewood, CO: Libraries Unlimited, 1989); and *Beyond the Library of the Future: More Alternative Futures for the Public Library* (Englewood, CO: Libraries Unlimited, 1997).

55. Roger E. Levien, *Confronting the Future: Strategic Visions for the 21st Century Public Library*, Policy Brief No. 4 (Chicago: American Library Association, 2011), 4, www.ala.org/ala/aboutala/offices/oitp/publications/ policybriefs/confronting_the_futu.pdf.

56. Ibid., 28. Reprinted with permission.

57. See, for instance, the American Library Association, Office for Information Technology Policy (OITP) Program, *America's Libraries for the 21st Century: An Annotated Bibliography* (Chicago: American Library Association, 2010). See also various writings of Clifford Lynch, Coalition for Networked Information, www.cni.org/about-cni/staff/clifford-a-lynch/publications/; "America's Libraries for the 21st Century: An Annotated Bibliography Version 0" (unedited draft of March 9, 2010), www.ala.org/offices/sites/ ala.org.offices/files/content/oitp/publications/policybriefs/future_of _libraries_biblio.pdf; and Paul Zenke, "The Future of Academic Libraries: An Interview with Steven J. Bell," *Education Futures*, March 26, 2012, www.educationfutures.com/2012/03/26/the-future-of-academic-libraries -an-interview-with-steven-j-bell/.

FUTURE VIEWS OF ACADEMIC LIBRARIES

It's too risky to NOT think differently, to NOT question our assumptions, to NOT design our futures.

—Jane Dysart

The Pew Research Center projects that, from 2005 to 2050, the U.S. population will increase from 296 million to 438 million, with 82 percent of that increase due to immigrants and their U.S.-born descendants.[1] As well, the nation's Hispanic and Asian populations are expected to triple by 2050, and by 2060 those groups currently labeled as minorities will form the new majority.

The U.S. Bureau of the Census reported that, in 2010, the number of people living in poverty was 46.2 million, up from 43.6 million in 2009—the fourth consecutive annual increase in the number of people in poverty.[2] At the same time, "the income of the typical American household fell 2.3 percent to $49,445—its third consecutive annual declines—capping a lost decade of stagnating earnings. Median household income hit its lowest level since 1996—$3,900 a year less than its peak in 1999."[3] As the new decade unfolds, the United States leads all developing nations in the overall percentage of children living in poverty, and child poverty has spread over the past decade from the metropolitan areas to the suburbs. Though children living in large cities are more likely to be poor, rural areas also struggle with children living in low-income households. The U.S. population is aging; the number of elderly people will increase substantially in the next twenty years and the number of people under forty-five will decrease. Because of the decrease of people who make up the bulk of the workforce (ages twenty-five to fifty-four), the United States is likely to face a shortfall of workers.

For at least the next thirty years, the western states will grow twice as fast as the national average, and the South will continue to be the most populated region in the nation. The Midwest and Northeast will grow at half the rate of the entire United States. At the same time, as the college attainment gap continues to widen with the most educated segment of the population reaching retirement age, the United States is likely to face an unprecedented shortage of college-educated workers by 2020. As Janet Lopez notes,

> Current projections indicate shifting demographics will create substantial increases in the population of American youth who historically have been the most poorly served, least economically successful and most under prepared for college level work. This, in conjunction with the retirement of the most well-educated population in the United States, will create a drop in education levels of U.S. workers. For our nation to retain a competitive advantage in the global marketplace, states must do a better job raising the educational levels of all ethnic/racial groups.[4]

Although educational attainment is universally rising, levels vary considerably across racial and ethnic lines. The rapid influx of students into community colleges will continue to increase, and those students will likely include, among others, displaced workers seeking to recareer, returning veterans, recent high school graduates, students needing developmental coursework, students seeking advanced placement, and older individuals seeking personal interest courses. The cost of obtaining an undergraduate degree will remain a challenge for many individuals and their families.

Complicating matters,

> Jobs of the future will increasingly rely on the types of skills
> that higher education develops. By 2018, 13.8 million new jobs
> will be created, 63% of which will require a college degree.
> . . . However, an estimated 3 million of these jobs will remain
> unclaimed simply because not enough workers will possess . . .
> [the necessary skills and education]. Sixty percent of adults—
> some 75 million people between the ages of 18 and 84—have
> no postsecondary credentials. . . . Traditional college-aged stu-
> dents will not graduate from college in large enough numbers
> to bridge this gap. To ensure that sufficient numbers of workers
> earn college degrees, many more adult students—also known
> as working learners—need to pursue higher education.[5]

Higher Education

There are more than seven thousand institutions of higher education in
the United States, and that number continues to increase. The Carnegie
Commission on Higher Education (http://carnegiefoundation.org) has
classified these institutions into various subdivisions according to the
highest degree offered:

Associate colleges. They offer all degrees at the associate level, or
bachelor's degrees comprise less than 10 percent of all undergraduate degrees.

Baccalaureate colleges. Baccalaureate degrees represent at least 10 percent of all undergraduate degrees, and fewer than fifty master's degrees
or twenty doctoral degrees are awarded during the time specified.

Master's colleges and universities. They awarded at least fifty master's degrees and fewer than twenty doctoral degrees during the time specified.

Doctorate-granting universities. They awarded at least twenty research doctoral degrees during the time specified.

Special focus institutions. They award baccalaureate or higher-level degrees where a high concentration of degrees (above 75 percent) is in a single field or set of related fields. Examples include faith-related institutions; medical schools; schools of engineering; schools of art, music, and design; schools of business and management; and law schools.

Tribal colleges. These are members of the American Indian Higher Education Consortium.

The Classification of Instructional Programs (CIP), produced by the National Center for Education Statistics and included as part of the Integrated Postsecondary Education Data System (IPEDS), provides a taxonomic scheme that tracks and reports different fields of study.[6] Institutions might be public or private, land grant (at public research intensive universities), for-profit, largely providing Internet-delivered educational programs, or have campuses in other countries. There are also a few institutions that have a combined academic and public library (likely called joint-use libraries). For instance, the King Library merges the main San José (Calif.) Public Library and the library of San José State University.

According to *Inside Higher Ed*, state support of higher education in 2010–2011 declined 0.7 percent from the previous year. Only nine states have actually cut their support in the past five years, with these five states reporting the deepest cuts: South Carolina (-11.3 percent), Rhode Island (-10.8 percent), Michigan (-7.1 percent), Arizona (-4.4 percent), and Idaho (-4.1 percent).[7] Further cuts are anticipated for the next fiscal year.

The *Almanac of Higher Education, 2011–12*, a special edition of the *Chronicle of Higher Education*, and *Global Recession and Universities*, a report of Moody's Investor Services, show the impact of the economic recession on academe. Some institutions expect students, staff, and faculty to serve as a buffer against financial losses. This means increasing tuitions, greater pressure to ensure that student enrollment does not drop (any drop might translate into a budget deficit), and no salary increases for faculty and staff, who instead will absorb increases in their contributions to health care and perhaps other benefits. With the cost of private higher education increasing faster than family income for 90 percent of U.S. families, the earnings value of some degrees compared to their price is decreasing; an exception is chemical engineering, which is still a good return on investment. State legislators and governors, as well as Congress and the president of the United States, are applying pressure to curtail tuition costs and to make institutions more accountable for the quality of education they deliver. State support for public institutions has declined while the number of students with financial needs has increased. "Private colleges spent a record 42.4 percent of their total tuition-and-fee income on aid for first time freshmen in 2010, up from 37.1 percent in 2000. But the higher discount rate (net financial aid as a percentage of net published tuition) leaves institutions with less cash to cover their operating needs."[8]

Institutions are seeking alterative sources of funding to offset their increased costs. Those sources might include the state and philanthropy. The report from Moody's describes the significant uncertainties and long-term trends in state funding. The states often are not in a position to contribute more than they do. With some states lessening their support as a percentage of the entire university budget, "flagship public universities are trying to disentangle themselves from their obligations to the states that created them." They might want greater flexibility in setting tuition rates, might enroll more students from out of the state or nation, and might express interest in privatization.[9] There is heightened competition for philanthropic dollars among public and private institutions.

On the positive side, endowment values, which declined sharply during the recession, climbed 8 percent in 2010. Colleges are beginning to view innovation as a way to experiment with new technology and greater collaboration among faculty, departments, and units such as libraries. The goal is more efficiency in programs and services.

In 2010, *USA Today* reported that one-third of first-year college students needed remedial course work in reading and math. Moreover, "students who need remedial classes are also more likely to drop out: Those taking any remedial reading, for example, had a 17% chance of completing a bachelor's degree."[10] Add to this startling statistic the fact that many high school and other students have a poor knowledge of U.S. and world history and world geography. Still, for those attending college, technological innovation will likely continue to change the way faculty teach and students learn. Distance education will remain important as academic institutions expand their student population globally, meet the learning goals of students in a cost-efficient manner, and accelerate corporate-academic partnerships. For many institutions distance and adult education is perceived as a way to compete internationally and reduce costs as class sizes become larger.

Emily Thomas, in an interesting blog posting, notes that the higher education landscape is rapidly changing and has come up with twenty-five predictions for the university of the future. Among these are sustainability, more green majors, green campuses, green-oriented common curriculum, and a shift to focus on local community.[11] Chapter 9, which picks up on some of the themes that Thomas notes, shows that some attention now focuses on scenarios for higher education and for municipal government. Such scenarios provide an important context to the types of library scenarios highlighted in this book.

Trends in Academic Libraries

It is common for academic institutions to reduce—often dramatically— the size of the budget allocated to their libraries. Although California did not make the list of states with the deepest budget cuts (see note 7), the University of California–Berkeley Library received an 18 percent cut in 2010. As a result, the library reduced its collections budget by 11 percent. The Stanford University Libraries cut its budget 15 percent, and the University of Washington Libraries' cut was 12 percent, or $3.636 million. With such cuts, libraries might reduce the number of hours open, perhaps on the weekend. They might merge departments; streamline services; eliminate print subscriptions for materials that can be found online; cancel journal and database subscriptions; cease unnecessary purchases of duplicate books; reduce binding, shelving, and storage of materials; close some branch libraries; lay off some employees; offer senior employees, both librarians and staff, buyouts to retire; and eliminate vacant positions.

Given such situations, combined with customer preferences for electronic access to materials, the inability to sustain comprehensive collections financially, and the likelihood that the near future will bring additional budget pressures, there is increased focus on customer demand setting the foundation for collection growth. It is clear that collaboration within and outside institutions will expand.[12]

At the same time, there is increased effort to link libraries and their institutions to environmental sustainability or the green movement, which, among other things, seeks greater energy efficiency, waste reduction, material conservation, and indoor environmental quality. Larry Hardesty points out that

> the academic library building is often the largest single building on a campus, and it frequently operates the longest hours of any campus building—even 24 hours a day at some institutions. Therefore, in these days of economic stress and growing environmental awareness, it is reasonable to scrutinize the costs of sustaining the library building. Are there more economical and environmentally friendly ways to heat, cool, light, and control the humidity of the library building?
>
> The academic library building is also the scene of considerable activity that also merits scrutiny as we become increasingly aware of the limited nature of the resources of our planet. For example, historically, academic libraries have served as places for the accumulation of . . . lots and lots of papers. . . . The production of paper is one of the more energy intensive industrial processes.[13]

Libraries can contribute to sustainability, for example, by using recycled paper and energy-saving lights, having a green roof with plants that filter rain water and insulate the building to reduce energy consumption, using lighter coats of paint to reflect the sun's heat and make rooms brighter to reduce the need for artificial light, installing compact fluorescent lights and motion-activated lights, and using waterless urinals and low-flush toilets. Hardesty concludes by noting that the "library . . . can lead the way in serving as an important symbol of the institution's commitment to environmental sustainability." Clearly, regardless of the preferred scenario, the vision that scenario identifies must be achieved through sustainability.

One knowledgeable observer of the academic library scene, David Lewis, has suggested that by 2020 the following will likely be true:[14]

- Google will have digitized nearly 100 million books. The contents of these books will be available through Google.
- All interested parties will have reached a court-approved process for charging for the use of in-copyright works.
- All published content will be delivered electronically. Most individuals will use an e-book reader or tablet to download content, and a printed book will be made available on a print-on-demand basis.
- Print repositories, managed by library consortiums, will house multiple copies of previously published materials.
- Open access will become the dominate model for scholarly journal publishing.
- Successful university presses will have evolved into broader university publishing units.
- A variety of open, often collaborative, scholarly communication mechanisms will be developed.

He goes on to suggest that academic libraries will need to deconstruct library print collections, move from item-by-item book selection to purchase-on-demand and subscriptions, manage the transition to open-access journals, curate the unique, and develop new mechanisms to fund national infrastructure.

Unfamiliarity with Libraries and the Role of Librarians

As is widely recognized, students prefer to use digital library resources, even if they are already in the library. They may not be aware that the digital resources they use are provided by the library. Complicating matters, they tend "to overuse Google and misuse scholarly databases. They preferred simple database searches to other methods of discovery, but generally exhibited 'a lack of understanding of search logic' that often foiled their attempts to find good sources." Furthermore,

> Students rarely ask librarians for help, even when they need
> it. The idea of a librarian as an academic expert who is avail-
> able to talk about assignments and hold their hands through
> the research process is, in fact, foreign to most students. Those
> who even have the word "librarian" in their vocabularies often
> think library staff are only good for pointing to different sec-
> tions of the stacks.[15]

As shown by Ithaka S + R, there may be a difference between how
the faculty views the library and how librarians view themselves:
librarians may see the library as serving primarily a teaching function,
whereas faculty see it primarily as a purchasing agent. Furthermore,
there is a perception that libraries have insufficiently engaged in "strategic planning to meet user needs for services and optimally manage
collections." The teaching of information literacy skills still reaches a
few faculty members and their students. Librarians continue to try to
convince faculty to partner with them and increase the information
fluency of college students, and, when librarians engage in such activities, faculty members do not always perceive it as teaching.[16] Accreditation organizations, both institutional and program, might see information literacy as a student learning outcome applicable to programs
and institutions as a whole. Naturally, not all programs and institutions
favor information literacy as an outcome; some, however, apparently
do. Yet librarians persist in viewing information literacy at the course
level. Treating it as a program or institutional goal requires a restructuring of library services and personnel and a partnership between
librarians and program faculty. Some of the following scenarios provide that restructuring.

Exploring the Use of Different Scenarios

Building from the scenarios presented in the previous chapters, we
developed a companion set that builds on new service roles libraries are
developing.[17] Our goal was to generate a set of scenarios that provide
a wide range of choices to academic libraries while still enabling them
to fine-tune their preferred future to the local situation. Any portrayal

of the near future will build on the present, but key elements might not be dramatically different than what libraries are presently doing. Still, the set must provide opportunities for libraries to move incrementally or dramatically in new directions.

Some of the scenarios recognize that libraries are seeking new ways to assist scholarly work of faculty members and to gain broader support for their role; librarians want greater recognition than their role as managers of bibliographic data at a time when universities want to "develop more integrated systems to monitor and manage the research outputs and performance of their researchers."[18]

Although Dana Mietzner and Guido Reger recommend that the number of proposed scenarios not exceed four, we offer two additional ones to give readers more choices from which to select. The fifth scenario focuses more on scholarly communication, and the the sixth makes the library an active partner in knowledge creation and data curation. Each of the six scenarios meet the Mietzner and Reger criteria, namely, plausibility (each is capable of happening), differentiation (each differs from the others, and together they offer multiple futures), decision-making utility (each offers insights into the future that help in planning and decision making), and challenging (each challenges conventional wisdom about the future).[19]

The following assumptions were made in the construction of the scenarios. First, the aftermath of the 2008–2009 economic recession will persist for several more years and will likely slow the expansive nature of any idealistic scenarios and the reaction of library directors to them. As well, institutional budgets have decreased, especially the part devoted to academic affairs, while the number of administrators ironically increased. Second, many libraries are likely to have a smaller workforce and to engage in staffing and operations reengineering. As the critical knowledge, abilities, and skill set that library directors expect of their workforce change, a smaller percentage of librarians will perhaps have the master's degree from a program accredited by the ALA. Third, the service expectations of faculty and students will likely increase. Fourth, the pace of technological innovation in libraries will not diminish; in fact, it might accelerate. Fifth, any set of scenarios needs to explore new service roles; the changing role of, and access to, collections in meeting information needs; staff transformation and the redesign of positions; repurposing of facilities to expand collaborate space; and recognizing the transformational role of information technology. Sixth, the content of the scenarios should build on current trends and not represent a total departure from what some libraries are doing. Seventh, instead of making each scenario completely different, some might logically build from previous ones.[20]

And, finally, forecaster Joseph P. Martino advises that a set of scenarios should project no more than fifteen years. He notes that the accuracy in predicting declines dramatically with a longer time frame.[21] Nevertheless, change seems to be accelerating; any projections past ten years are more likely susceptible to external forces, such as a reoccurrence of an economic recession. Between now and, let us say 2027, there will likely be more than one recession, perhaps set off by monetary events in Europe or Asia, that directly affect the U.S. economy. If we extend the scenarios to a larger time frame, it is impossible to make meaningful projections. After all, how many in the profession in the early 1980s would have projected the environment of today? Still, we probed for some general trends.

Six Academic Library Scenarios

SCENARIO ONE: THE PRESENT IS THE FUTURE

Although there has been no increase in the library's budget or the size of the professional workforce for years, the library retains a traditional commitment to support print and digital collections but tips the balance in favor of the latter. The staff recognizes that students rely heavily on databases, read/use digital content, and seldom use the library's OPAC. The library retains its traditional services (circulation, reference, and ILL) but adds digital components to them, namely, the capability of remote and on-site library users to ask questions via text messaging and the library's home page and receive prompt responses, engage in self-checkout, and place ILL requests online. The library reallocates staff to new positions and defines accountability in terms of the amount and quality of service it provides to students and faculty, its support of classroom instruction, and customer satisfaction. The library manages the institutional repository and partners with the writing center and tutorial services, among other campus services, perhaps through a learning or other type of commons.

The primary motivation for this scenario is to meet the institutional mission with the expectation of an online environment that supplements traditional campus life. Digital services continue to expand. Undoubtedly the library is wireless, and there might be an information or learning commons; however, these do not affect the service role the library director envisions.

SCENARIO TWO: PRESS A BUTTON LIBRARY

With the increased digital availability of information resources from an increasing array of service providers, this virtual library sees its primary role as mediator of content licenses. Still, librarians interact with students by digital communication devices and in virtual spaces including online gaming. All students have e-reading devices, which are also personal communication devices through which they can read on a screen, project and read on any surface, and capture in print or transfer to computer by touch. To support the educational programs, the library maintains contracts with vendors or other libraries to provide support services (e.g., digital reference service or full-text, online journals).

The primary motivation for this scenario is to acknowledge that the management of physical objects is no longer a primary activity and that students and faculty located remotely need online access to many materials available in the library. Additionally, there is a desire to convert precious campus (library) space to support classroom learning more directly and to relieve space congestion on campus. The institution is greatly expanding distance and adult education, defined in terms of web delivery of content.

SCENARIO THREE: THE LIBRARY IS A LEARNING ENTERPRISE

The library has a professional staff specializing in learning pedagogy and partnering with classroom faculty in teaching information and visual literacy competencies, working collaboratively with support services across the campus such as through learning or knowledge commons, and engaging in evaluation and assessment to improve the quality of the services offered and student learning. The assessment occurs at the institutional level, with the library participating in the achievement of program and institutional student learning outcomes. To do this the library redirects staff to work closely with the academic programs as part of a collaborative research team and no longer offers individualized instruction in the classroom that merely supports classroom evaluation or assessment. The library combines a technologically advanced learning environment with inviting instruction space, classrooms, and support services (e.g., writing tutors). Librarians also make "office calls," perhaps by Skype or by visiting dormitories and dining halls. Webinars make distant interactions and collaborations available anytime, anyplace. The library might also manage the institutional repository.

The primary motivations for pursing this scenario are to make the library more of an institutional partner that accomplishes the educational mission and vision the institution projects. The goal is to make the library an important player in attracting and retaining students, in assisting faculty in their teaching, and in collaborating with faculty on funded research projects. Achievement of this scenario might necessitate a professional staff with an assortment of advanced degrees.

SCENARIO FOUR: EXPANDING SERVICE ROLES
(ESPECIALLY THOSE EXTERNAL TO THE LIBRARY)

The library assures seamless access to needed information and data in an environment that emphasizes the library as a designer of information systems and a service provider. Networks and cooperative arrangements provide backup support and achieve savings in bibliographic control and access to needed resources. The library has greatly downsized its physical collections and traditional services. In fact, it increasingly contracts services such as circulation and e-reserves, from larger cooperatives that exists at a national level. (The goal is to expand the digital collection and downsize the paper collection while assuming new service roles.)

The physical space emphasizes group and individual study space and sharing space with selected campus support units (e.g., the writing center). Moving beyond the physical setting of the library, four types of service roles for librarians emerge as they serve as partners to teaching, learning, and research:

1. Embedded specialists support faculty research teams and projects and develop systems to preserve or provide access to their research and the library collection. These specialists might preserve data sets that faculty members produce and make them accessible online. They might also convert faculty field notes and photographic collections for online access as well as assist faculty in a web-based sharing of resources with their colleagues at other institutions.

2. Librarians work in a center for digital initiatives, which produces digital content for use in campus scholarship and teaching, digitizes signature collections from the library's special collections, and offers consultative services to academic units undertaking digital projects.

3. Embedded instructional design librarians work closely with academic programs to support mutually agreed-on student learning outcomes that contribute to student learning and faculty teaching, especially in the online delivery of courses and curriculum. These librarians include information literacy, broadly defined to cover visual literacy, in their program-level instruction to contribute to the institution's successful methodology for addressing general education learning outcomes. The library strives to move beyond course-level instruction and embrace an educational role at the program level.

4. Librarians might be engaged in special projects such as working with the specialists and instructional design librarians to develop digital guides as finding aids and help guides.

The same librarians might perform all of these roles or a subset of them depending on resources available. With this scenario the library assumes an active, nurturing role of information discovery, supporting and advancing teaching and learning pedagogy, and producing knowledge for the institution. In fact, with the changing nature of knowledge creation and use, the library is an active partner in the institutional effort to support research projects irrespective of organizational (i.e., public, private, and for-profit), geographic, and national boundaries. Embedding does not mean merely passive presence in academic departments; embedding librarians must be proactive.

To accommodate the service roles, the library further outsources services related to the management of collections and no longer offers assistance at a traditional regularly staffed reference desk. Students and others needing research assistance either make appointments with knowledgeable staff members or convey their questions electronically to the library.

The primary motivations for pursuing this scenario are (a) to build relationships with faculty and other stakeholders, (b) to perform different roles (face-to-face, digital, tutorial, and pre-assessment), (c) to adjust to the changing information needs and information-seeking behavior of faculty and students, and (d) to expand the critical role the library actively plays in student learning and research. The library is engaged in reengineering operations and staff positions. Given the expectation of accreditation organizations, the library has dramatically shifted its attention to program-level assessment for all students wherever and however they participate. The library advances the institutional mission and how it demonstrates campus-wide support while coping with the shift in student use of databases over the library's OPAC. Depending on the extent to which a library assumes the four service roles without having staff engaged in more than one service role, there is likely a need to expand the number of professional staff members, though not necessarily librarians who hold accredited master's degrees.

SCENARIO FIVE: THE LIBRARY AS THE CAMPUS SCHOLARLY COMMUNICATION PUBLISHER

Building from either the first or third scenario, the library, which provides a service-oriented infrastructure that relies on digital technologies and shared ideas to build and sustain communities that exist beyond the home campus, facilitates the flow, organization, and repackaging of information. It also views scholarly communication (the process of conducting research and sharing the results: from creation to dissemination and preservation of knowledge for the purposes of teaching, research, and scholarship) as part of its core mission and actively engages in electronic publishing on behalf of academic departments, faculty, and graduate students. To accomplish this role, the library invests in the tools necessary to engage in publishing, preferring to take a more independent role, and develops both the infrastructure and expertise as an online publisher. The library creates new business models that encourage cross-institutional cooperation.

As a complement, the library advises academic units, faculty, and graduate students about choices for placement of their scholarly, research, and classroom teaching materials. The library integrates the university press, institutional repository, coverage of intellectual property rights, and publishing (online and print). It is also involved in technology transfer and advises the university on international technology transfer. There may be a need to expand the number of professional staff members, though not necessarily librarians who hold accredited master's degrees from a program accredited by the ALA.

The primary motivations for pursuing this scenario are to ensure that the university effectively addresses scholarly communication and changing publishing models and protects its intellectual assets. The goal is to make the library more central to the dissemination and preservation of campus scholarship and research. A concern is the institution's tenure and review process as the faculty move into nontraditional scholarly publishing. To achieve this scenario, the library director may assume a broader institutional role, namely, managing the information infrastructure (including information technologies).

SCENARIO SIX: THE LIBRARY AS A MORE ACTIVE RESEARCH PARTNER

Building from the previous two scenarios and the library's role in knowledge creation, scholarly access to information and data, and data curation through its infrastructure and services, the library becomes an active partner in research, including e-science, e-social sciences, and e-humanities, irrespective of geographic (national, too) boundaries. The library develops departmental, cross-discipline, and cross-departmental relationships with faculty and departments engaged in large-scale, funded, interdisciplinary research projects to make research findings and data sets widely available. Librarians serve as members of research teams charged with preserving data and making them accessible to the larger research community. There may be a need to expand the number of professional staff members, though not necessarily librarians who hold accredited master's degrees from a program accredited by the ALA.

The primary motivation for pursuing this scenario is the changing nature of knowledge creation and use in a research-intensive institution. With the federal government and other funding bodies expecting data sets and papers produced from their funding to be preserved for use by others, there is increased demand for the expertise librarians can bring to research teams.

Through in-person and telephone interviews with twelve library directors at baccalaureate-, master's-, and doctoral-granting institutions, we refined the scenarios and their relevance to a diverse set of institutions. The goal was to build on what others had suggested but not to create a definitive set of scenarios; rather, we see the set as forming a discussion document. It was noted that scenarios five and six may not have universal application. They might also be selected as part of another scenario. Further, scenario one may be unacceptable to such libraries, if they do not not engage in the full range of activities that research universities envision as an essential role for the institution moving forward.

Other points raised include that the fourth scenario might include the concept of the library terrace, space located near dormitories but enabling librarians to interact with students through Internet messaging on mobile devices and to work with students in comfortable study space that might have access to computers. The space definitely does not contain books and or support the traditional image of a library and instruction in information literacy. Library staff might be in the space at allocated times to work with students on a one-to-one basis.[22] As more college libraries respond to the mandate that higher education prepare students to enter the workforce, especially by providing vocational education; vocational majors are less likely to engage in broad reading, preferring to consult sources such as manuals, to read less widely, and to rely on online information.

Libraries serving liberal arts institutions might focus on the fourth scenario. However, whether they adopt that scenario or another one, they are likely to include a larger role for printed materials, especially if there are courses and programs covering the history of the book, book arts, and creative uses of the book. Such courses most likely cover both print and digital materials, enabling students to make comparisons. For them, in essence, special collections or the college archives become a source for teaching and learning, and perhaps not as much (or not at all) for research. Further, libraries might add a component to any given scenario for an academic commons where faculty and students can deposit the results of their scholarly work and research and for faculty, information technologists, librarians, and other academic professionals to form a community to share knowledge, develop collaborations, and disseminate digital tools and innovative practices. Such a space also encourages peer-to-peer learning and creativity in an inviting space.

In brief, liberal arts colleges will continue to focus on how the tools, methods, and communication practices of the digital age will enhance the education they provide. Libraries in these institutions will explore methods and practices to improve learning and help faculty challenge students in their course work and scholarship. They will also combine digital modes of communication with in-person learning and use information technology to help students work creatively and collaboratively, make sense of massive amounts of data, and make increasing use of print and digital archives and special collections.

The availability of digital resources has many scholars quite excited. For example, an Australian humanities scholar maintains that "this is a pivotal point of change in the humanities. Those who do not want to be part of it [i.e., digital research] now will be left behind. Those who do will have the privilege of being part of the most exciting and transformative period in the history of humanities."[23]

Extending the Scenarios beyond Fifteen Years

When asked about changes to the scenarios beyond fifteen years, the directors surveyed noted that there will likely be mergers of institutional libraries, such as combinations of academic and public libraries or of two or more academic libraries. A merger might result in combined staff and digital services. The goal is to minimize duplication of effort while improving service efficiency and effectiveness. There is a feeling that, in the future, institutions cannot commit to the same economy of scale that they did in the past with a library and the costs associated with its collections, staff, technology, and facilities. The merger, therefore, represents forced efficiency on institutional libraries. In addition, there will be new opportunities for collaboration, as well as outsourced services.

There will also be changes with the OPAC, and these will be more associated with institutional asset control. Library customers will most likely use the OPAC to see if the library holds a particular source. Libraries will increasingly rely on services such as Serial Solutions Summon and the EBSCO Discovery Service, both web-based unified discovery services, and such services may facilitate further staff reallocation. As this example recognizes, the way people consult and seek information will likely continue to change. Libraries are declining in importance as a place to go for information, whether through OPACs or reference staff, and writings about data or information literacy outside the profession often fail to recognize what librarians hope to achieve. Librarians may be putting energy and good thought into building authoritative systems of indexed information and scholarly, vetted information, but customer demand, even in academe, may be changing. After all, many see Google Scholar as a good enough discovery tool.

Libraries might come to view consortia differently and use them as a method to engage in cooperative collection management. The purpose would be to retain fewer copies of trade publications, especially those no longer needed for course reserve and university press publications. With reduced collections of duplicate material, space might be used for other purposes.

Surprisingly, especially at some colleges, not all students rely on digital content and means of electronic communication (e.g., smartphones). They are comfortable with print resources, and there is a concern that many e-books go unused and do not share the same platform; there are differences among publishers. Further, e-textbooks are not as inexpensive as first thought. Some college directors believe these patterns will not change in the foreseeable future.

Librarians will devote more time to developing working relationships with faculty, and those relationship will create new instructional roles for librarians, especially those having a teaching, pedagogical, and assessment background. There will be increased pressure on faculty to engage in effective teaching since higher education prizes effective teaching and learning and stakeholders (e.g., government) are concerned about the cost and quality of a degree. In brief, libraries will engage even more in cooperative relationships and not be stand-alone organizations that many once were. In part, a focus of those cooperative relationships will be on adjunct faculty, a group increasing in numbers at some institutions.

There will be continued pressure at many colleges and universities to redesign space and for libraries to redesign building space to move units engaged in study skills (e.g., writing centers) into their physical space. The result will be expansion of learning, academic, and other types of commons. There will also be redesign of circulation and reference areas to promote individual assistance, when necessary. Related to this change is the fact that, in states such as Pennsylvania, librarians are no longer included in many public high schools. This means that students enter college without an understanding of the role of libraries or an introduction to information literacy. How will academe reach out to students and convert them into effective and efficient library users?

Another change will be to library staff. As director James G. Neal explained, speaking about ARL libraries, "Academic libraries now hire an increasing number of individuals to fill professional librarian positions who do not have the master's degree in library science. Instead of appointing librarians with the traditional qualifying credential, they hire staff to fill librarian positions who hold a variety of qualifications, such as advanced degrees in subject disciplines, specialized language skills, teaching experience, or technology expertise."[24]

This trend is not confined to research universities. More professional staff may not have the traditional master's LIS degree and may come from fields such as computer engineering, instructional technology, marketing, donor relations, and education with a specialty of pedagogy, archiving (e.g., digital archivists), and business administration (holding the master's degree). Those in business administration will be engaged in analyzing the library as a business and in activities such as analyzing risk and return on investment. The challenge will be to integrate them into the workforce in a way that they are seen as part of the professional staff, not support staff. There will also be a blending of responsibilities, ranging from the traditional (e.g., reference service) to the nontraditional—such as the formation of a new "creative services and outreach" department that combines marketing and donor relations. Clearly, the LIS master's will form only one path for those working in libraries in professional positions, and even these professionals will continue to expand their skill set. What all of this means for universities where the professional staff enjoy promotion and tenure remains to be seen.

Whether or not they have a master's degree, James L. Mullins, in a study of research universities, shows a preference for professional staff who are people-centered and comfortable dealing with faculty, administrators, and students in various academic departments.[25]

Concluding Thoughts

It is important to remind readers that librarians can (and probably would) select elements from different scenarios as individual libraries create their preferred scenario. For our purposes, as several library directors who read the scenarios commented, the set provokes thinking about a relevant future and encourages managerial leaders and stakeholders to revisit the library's mission and vision statement. Before settling on a particular scenario or a hybrid, we encourage readers to review the discussion of general trends and to supplement such information with what is available from their local institution, including any strategic plan SWOT analysis compiled by the college or university, town or city. Box 5.1 offers examples of the types of questions a SWOT analysis covers.

SWOT Analysis Sample Questions

INTERNAL STRENGTHS

- Does the institution have a positive reputation in the external community?
- Do those who interact with members of the institution find the experience positive?
- What proactive partnerships exist with other academic institutions, businesses and corporations, and funding agencies?
- What do accreditation organizations, either program and institutional, say about the institution and its various units?
- To what extent do the institution and its programs meet student learning goals?
- How large are classes, and how does class size affect the ability to meet those learning goals?
- How many years does it take to graduate?
- Do faculty and staff support the campus mission?
- What services support studies, and how effective are they?
- Are facilities new and well maintained, and are buildings attractive?
- Is the campus friendly and safe?
- How diverse are the student body, faculty, staff, and administration?
- Is the faculty dedicated to student learning?
- Is the faculty nationally and internationally recognized in certain areas of teaching and research?
- Is there healthy shared governance?
- Are external boards strong, supportive, and active?
- Is the residential campus modern and attractive?
- Are artistic and cultural performances (concerts/seminars/exhibits), as well as stimulating speakers, available on a regular basis?

INTERNAL WEAKNESSES

- Is the operational structure/bureaucracy ineffective?
- Is there fiscal uncertainty?
- Is there a match between research expectation and support?
- Are there high and unequal workloads for faculty and staff?
- Do departments have the ability to hire and retain faculty?
- How well prepared are students when they enter the institution?

- Is there a highly competitive market for diverse faculty and staff?
- Do administrative reporting requirements absorb a large percentage of resources?
- Is the percentage of student retention and students transferring to the institution higher than in past years?

EXTERNAL OPPORTUNITIES

- What partnerships exist in support of university initiatives?
- What are the expanded possibilities for students to enter the workforce while they are students and after they graduate?
- Is there a match between curricular and societal interests?
- Is there increased demand for mid-career redirection and lifelong learning?
- Is there increased interest in global initiatives and in technological advances?
- Is the pool of future students increasing locally and regionally?

EXTERNAL THREATS

- If the institution is public, is there a state budget crisis?
- What is the response to program and student scheduling demands?
- Is there an increase in reporting expected by government and society?
- Is there a shift in focus on numerical achievement versus qualitative achievement?
- Is public perception of the institution and its programs positive or negative?
- Is there local competition from other colleges and universities in the area, or from online programs?
- Is there a societal and student perception of education as solely a means to a job?
- Is administrative reporting perceived as a ritual and meaningless?
- Do reporting requirements absorb a large percentage of resources?
- How familiar are the external community and the institution's board of governance with higher education? Does that board perceive the institution from purely a business perspective?

The answers to any of these questions might mean recategorization as a strength, weakness, opportunity, or threat.

Lesson 1: The future creates the present.
Lesson 2: The people we see in 2020 will look quite different from today.
Lesson 3: Great technology revolutions are yet to come.
Lesson 4: Socially and economically the way it is, is not the way it will be.
Lesson 5: A vision must be compelling to make a difference.
Lesson 6: Futuring increases uncertainty, at least for a while.
Lesson 7: Everything possible today was at one time impossible.
Lesson 8: Everything impossible today may at some time in the future be possible.
—*Glen Hiemstra*

NOTES

1. Pew Research Center, "U.S. Population Projections: 2005–2050" (2008), http://pewsocialtrends.org/2008/02/11/us-population-projections-2005-2050/. These are, however, merely projections; unstated variables (e.g., war, plague, global economy) will likely influence actual outcomes.

2. Bureau of the Census, "Poverty: Highlights" (2011), www.census.gov/hhes/www/poverty/about/overview/index.html.

3. "The Cost of Inaction," *New York Times*, September 14, 2011, A28.

4. Janet Lopez, *The Impact of Demographic Changes on United States Higher Education 2000–2050* (2006), http://sheeo.org/pubs/demographics-lopez.pdf.

5. Courtney L. Vien, "The Multi-generational Student Body: National Study Sheds Light on Adult Student Retention," *Almanac of Higher Education, 2011–12, Chronicle of Higher Education* 57, no. 1 (August 26, 2011), 19.

6. IPEDS provides basic data that describe postsecondary education, in terms of the numbers of students enrolled, staff employed, dollars expended, and degrees earned. For the suite of IPEDS data services, see http://nces.ed.gov/ipeds/.

7. Scott Jaschik, "The Sinking States," *Inside Higher Ed*, January 24, 2011, www.insidehighered.com/news/2011/01/24/states_make_more_cuts_in_spending_on_higher_education. Surprisingly, despite all of its budget cuts, California did not rank among the five.

8. See *Almanac of Higher Education, 2011–12*; Moody's Investor Service, *Global Recession and Universities: Funding Strains to Keep Up with Rising Demand* (2009), http://globalhighered.files.wordpress.com/2009/07/s-globrecess-univ-6-09.pdf; Rachel Wiseman, "Hunkering Down, Colleges Rethink Financial Strategies," *Almanac of Higher Education, 2011–12*, 6.

9. Kevin Carey, "Why Flagship Public Universities Should Stay Public," *Chronicle of Higher Education*, August 12, 2011, A64.

10. "One-Third of Students Need Remedial College Math, Reading," *USA Today*, May 11, 2010, www.usatoday.com/news/education/2010 -05-11-remedial-college_N.htm.

11. Emily Thomas, "25 Predictions for the University of the Future," *Associates Degree*, July 25, 2009, www.associatesdegree.com/2009/07/29/25 -predictions-for-the-university-of-the-future/.

12. See Peter Hernon and Ronald R. Powell, *Convergence and Collaboration of Campus Information Services* (Westport, CT: Libraries Unlimited, 2008).

13. Larry Hardesty, "The Environmental Sustainability of Academic Libraries," *Library Issues: Briefings for Faculty and Administrators* 32, no. 1 (September 2011), www.libraryissues.com/sub/LI320001.asp

14. David Lewis, "From Stacks to the Web: The Transformation of Academic Library Collecting," *College and Research Libraries*, prepublication preprint (anticipated publication date, January 2013).

15. Steve Kolowich, "What Students Don't Know," *Inside Higher Ed*, August 22, 2011, www.insidehighered.com/news/2011/08/22/erial_study_of _student_research_habits_at_illinois_university_libraries_reveals_alarmingly _poor_information_literacy_and_skills.

16. Matthew P. Long and Roger C. Schonfeld, *Ithaka S + R Library Survey 2010: Insights from U.S. Academic Library Directors* (New York: ITHAKA, 2010), 5, 41; available at www.sr.ithaka.org/research-publications/ library-survey-2010.

17. A set of four scenarios developed for use at the 19th Annual Conference on Libraries and the Future was reviewed by six directors of academic libraries. Those scenarios have been expanded and serve as the basis of this chapter. Long Island Library Resource Council, 19th Annual Conference on Libraries and the Future, "Imagine the Future" (Oakdale, NY: Dowling College, October 21–22, 2010), DVD. For the original set of scenarios, see Peter Hernon, Robert E. Dugan, and Danuta A. Nitecki, *Engaging in Evaluation and Assessment Research* (Santa Barbara, CA: Libraries Unlimited, 2011), 252–54.

18. John MacColl and Michael Judd, *Supporting Research: Environments, Administration and Libraries* (Dublin, OH: OCLC Research, 2011), 6, www.oclc.org/research/publications/library/2011/2011-10.pdf.

19. Dana Mietzner and Guido Reger, "Advantages and Disadvantages of Scenario Approaches for Strategic Foresight," *International Journal of Technology Intelligence and Planning* 1, no. 2 (2005), 233, www.lampsacus .com/documents/StragegicForesight.pdf.

20. For additional assumptions, see James L. Mullins, Frank R. Allen, and Jon R. Hufford, "Top Ten Assumptions for the Future of Academic Libraries: A Report from the ACRL Research Committee," *College and Research Libraries News* 68, no. 4 (April 2007): 240–41, 46.

21. Joseph P. Martino, "The Precision of Delphi Estimates," *Technological Forecasting* 1, no. 3 (1970): 293–99.

22. "Case in Part 6: Drexel University Libraries, United States: Learning Terraces," *LibraryConnect* (Amsterdam: Elsevier, March 2012); for more information, see chapter 6, "Toward Building an Embedded Academic Library."

23. Paul L. Arthur, "Virtual Strangers: E-research and the Humanities," *Australian Cultural History* 27, no. 1 (2009) 47–59.

24. James G. Neal, "Raised by Wolves: Integrating the New Generation of Feral Professionals into the Academic Library," *Library Journal*, February 15, 2006, www.libraryjournal.com/article/CA6304405.html.

25. James L. Mullins, "Are MLS Graduates Being Prepared for the Changing and Emerging Roles That Librarians Must Now Assume within Research Libraries?" *Journal of Library Administration* 52, no. 1 (2012): 124–32, http://dx.doi.org/10.1080/01930826.2011.629966.

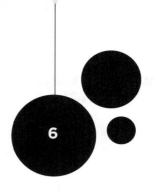

PERSPECTIVES ON TRENDS AND SCENARIOS: ACADEMIC LIBRARIES

Confront the brutal facts (yet never lose faith).

—Jim Collins, Good to Great

F or this chapter, we asked some library directors to comment on selected themes that have relevance to the set of scenarios depicted in chapter 5. For illustrative purposes, we focus on two themes: scholarly communication and space planning. One director provides an overview of scholarly communication but from the perspective of liberal arts colleges; a second director offers a different perspective on the same topic. The third director examines library space, and the final director discusses space planning and illustrates how the topic is linked to the previous set of scenarios.

Scholarly Communication and Liberal Arts College Libraries

BY RICHARD FYFFE

The early history of the scholarly communication reform movement is most closely associated with research-intensive universities and research libraries.[1] Four events, not entirely selected at random, mark the key themes that characterized this period. In 1991, Princeton University threatened cancellation, due to a large price increase, of all Pergamon journals, sparking debate and calls for further research into journal pricing policies and the reasons for price increases.[2] The next year, the Andrew Mellon Foundation published the study *University Libraries and Scholarly Communication*, which was followed in 1995 by Ann Okerson and James J. O'Donnell's edited volume of a widely discussed series of e-mail exchanges that debated Stevan Harnad's "radical proposal for the reform of scientific publishing."[3] Finally, in 1997, the Scholarly Publishing and Academic Resources Coalition (SPARC) was founded under the aegis of the ARL "to correct imbalances in the scholarly publishing system" by, as its strategy was at that time, encouraging development of not-for-profit competitors to high-priced scholarly journals.

The themes sounded in these events and initiatives include the conflict between the "gift economy" of scholarly publishing and the market economy of commercial publishing, the opportunities created by digital technology to return scholarly publishing to the academy where much of it is created, and a reexamination of the purpose of copyright protection in scholarly publishing (as distinct from commercial publishing). The STEM fields (science, technology, engineering, and mathematics) were the focus of attention during this period because prices in those fields were especially high and because digital technology had already begun transforming scholarly communication in these fields. As Paul Ginsparg, founder of the arXiv physics preprint server now based at Cornell University, recollected in a 1996 talk,

> The first database, hep-th (for High Energy Physics—Theory), was started in August of '91 and was intended for usage by a small subcommunity of less than 200 physicists, then working

on a so-called "matrix model" approach to studying string theory and two dimensional gravity. . . . Within a few months, the original hep-th had quickly expanded in its scope to over 1000 users, and after a few years had over 3800 users. More significantly, there are numerous other physics databases now in operation . . . that currently serve over 35,000 researchers and typically process more than 70,000 electronic transactions per day.[4]

Humanities departments in liberal arts colleges were also experimenting with scholarly digital publication at this time. The *Bryn Mawr Classical Review* has been published electronically since 1990, and the *Bryn Mawr Medieval Review* (now the *Medieval Review*) since 1993.[5]

Since those early years, the scholarly communications reform movement has broadened both its scope and its goals. It no longer focuses so directly on reducing the price of scholarly journal subscriptions (although high prices are still a challenge) or on returning scholarly publishing to nonprofit publishers and the academy. Scholarly communication, in addition to referring to the disciplinary practices that structure the dissemination of scholarly knowledge, has become shorthand for two meanings: on the one hand, it refers to an analytic "author/reader" framework that seeks critical understanding of the entire life cycle of scholarly knowledge and the connected roles of researchers, teachers, students, funders, libraries, publishers, and other kinds of agencies in the creation, dissemination, critique, reuse, and preservation of knowledge. And, on the other hand, it embraces a public policy advocacy framework that critically examines the economic and legal relationships that constrain or facilitate the creation and flow of scholarly knowledge, urging recognition that knowledge is a kind of commons, with each discovery or innovation dependent on the accomplishments of earlier scholars.[6]

In recent years, reform advocates have focused particularly on publicly funded research, arguing that the peer-reviewed papers derived from research funded at taxpayer expense ought to be accessible to the full taxpaying public, not just those affiliated with research universities. Many scholarly communication reform advocates have also urged greater openness in the dissemination of other products of the scholarly communication process, such as the primary data on which scholarly knowledge is based. The scholarly communication movement is thus closely allied with a broader openness movement that includes open data, open-source software, open educational materials, open teaching, and open courses.

NOT JUST RESEARCH I:
LIBRARY ARTS COLLEGES, UNDERGRADUATE LEARNING,
AND SCHOLARLY COMMUNICATION REFORM

Despite the strong connections between the scholarly communications reform movement and research universities/research libraries, the economic, technological, and cultural changes under way in scholarly publishing affect many types of higher education institutions. This section focuses on private liberal arts colleges and their libraries, which have a deep stake in the availability of scholarly literature and active engagement in efforts to illuminate and reform the scholarly publishing system. However, many of these points could be generalized to comprehensive state universities and community colleges. At the same time, the liberal arts sector is difficult to define precisely, and any generalizations across this sector are likely to go astray for significant numbers of these institutions.

One way of defining the sector (per Francis Oakley) is as "small college-universities devoted exclusively (or almost exclusively) to the teaching of undergraduates."[7] According to the classification used by the Carnegie Foundation for the Advancement of Teaching, ninety-eight institutions in the United States award at least 80 percent of their bachelor's degree majors in the arts and sciences and offer no graduate degrees in fields corresponding to undergraduate majors (A&S-F/NGC). An additional thirty-three institutions award at least 80 percent of their bachelor's degree majors in the arts and sciences but offer graduate degrees in up to half of the fields corresponding to undergraduate majors (A&S-F/SGC).[8] Eighty of these institutions are members of the Oberlin Group of Liberal Arts College Libraries (www.oberlingroup.org).

The focus on teaching in Oakley's definition can too easily mask the role of active research in faculty and student lives at liberal arts colleges, and hence the urgency for these institutions of the issues addressed by the scholarly communications reform movement. Like faculty at research universities, those at many liberal arts colleges are required to publish peer-reviewed scholarship to gain tenure, and many of them continue to be published after tenure, in some cases at rates similar to those of faculty at larger institutions. In the early 1990s, Robert A. McCaughey conducted "a discipline-by-discipline count of scholarly publications (books and articles) and citations of some 2,000 faculty at 24 colleges and four universities." The results, he writes, "suggested that many senior faculty at leading liberal arts colleges publish (and are cited) at rates approaching the mean level of publishing among their university peers, while a few exceeded it."

> A half dozen colleges had several departments whose senior members published at rates approaching department-specific university norms. To be sure, this was not true of all 24 colleges in the study, and even at colleges with the highest institutional levels of publication, a few faculty within individual departments often accounted for much of the total productivity. Still, at nearly all the colleges surveyed there was a cadre of faculty whose scholarly productivity approached that of university departments.[9]

Not just the faculty at liberal arts colleges are active researchers; students collaborate with their professors in their research, and liberal arts learning is frequently organized around research and the research process. Curricula in liberal arts colleges are typically based on inquiry that draws on primary research materials (e.g., laboratory experiments, field station observations, archival research) rather than on textbooks. One consequence of this inquiry-centered approach to learning is the important role of liberal arts colleges in preparing students for graduate study. The Nobel laureate Tom Cech, a graduate of Grinnell College, writes that "only about 8 percent of students who attend four-year colleges or universities are enrolled in baccalaureate colleges (a category that includes national liberal arts colleges). Among the students who obtain Ph.D.'s in science, 17 percent received their undergraduate degree at a baccalaureate college. Thus, these colleges are about twice as productive as the average institution in training eventual Ph.D.'s."[10]

THE SITUATION OF LIBERAL ARTS COLLEGE LIBRARIES: COLLECTIONS AND CONSORTIA

The library collections at liberal arts colleges and other undergraduate institutions have traditionally been distinguished in mission and kind from those at research libraries. As Larry Hardesty and Collette Mak wrote in 1994, librarians, faculty, and administrators traditionally assume that

> undergraduate library collections should be substantively different from research library collections. They should be built on different principles to serve a different type of patron. While research collections should have considerable diversity and depth reflecting the research interests of local scholars, undergraduate libraries should have a higher degree of similarity built around a core collection that serves the more limited needs of undergraduates.

Their article documented the distance between the actual character of library collections in liberal arts colleges and the "ideal" of a core collection but still called on librarians to "redouble their efforts to identify and acquire essential books that should form the 'core collection' of every undergraduate library."[11]

However, two forces at least will continue to undermine the concept of "core" in liberal arts college libraries, bridge the difference in kind (though not in scale) between college and research university library collections, and deepen the alliance between liberal arts colleges and other types of institutions in the scholarly communications arena. As undergraduate curricula in liberal arts colleges are increasingly oriented around the processes of research and inquiry—around the logic of discovery rather than the post hoc, textbook logic of explanation—the literature needed by students in their learning (no less than the literature needed by faculty) will be increasingly harder to predict, falling ever farther outside a predetermined "core."

Moreover, with the transition to electronic platforms largely complete for scholarly journals, liberal arts colleges are increasingly participating in consortial licensing of these materials along with larger institutions. Liberal arts college faculty and students have the same stake in unmediated, broad, stable, and enduring access to scholarly knowledge as the patrons of research libraries; all are bound into the same market dynamics. As a consequence, liberal arts college libraries are and will continue to be engaged in many of the same efforts as their colleagues in larger institutions to educate their communities about the political economy of scholarly communication, to create tools and practices that broaden access to scholarly knowledge, and to participate in public advocacy.

Campus-Based Open-Access Policies

Librarians in liberal arts colleges, like their counterparts in larger institutions, have taken the lead on their campuses in facilitating discussion and education on the challenges created by restricted access to scholarly knowledge and the open-access alternatives. With the involvement of librarians, the faculty at Trinity University (San Antonio), Oberlin College, Rollins College, Hope College, and others have passed open-access requirements that follow the so-called Harvard model, granting their institutions "permission to make his or her scholarly journal articles openly accessible in the College's institutional repository."[12] Open-access policies are commonly modeled on the one passed by the Faculty of Arts and Sciences at Harvard University in 2008, granting the university a nonexclusive right to make scholarly articles openly available through a campus repository and requiring each author to provide an electronic copy of the final version. Under this model, waivers are granted on request.[13]

Liberal arts college libraries have also hosted events on their campuses to mark international Open Access Week (www.openaccessweek .org). The Robert W. Woodruff Library–Atlanta University Center, for example, which serves Morehouse College, Spelman College, Clark Atlanta University, and the Interdenominational Theological Center, used Open Access Week in 2011 to convene a meeting of a representative group of faculty across all its constituent schools to initiate dialogue and activities. At Macalester College, the libraries raised awareness by sponsoring a prize drawing for Amazon Kindles for students, faculty, and staff who submitted correct answers to a daily quiz on open-access issues.[14]

Repository Development and Online Journals

Many liberal arts colleges have developed digital repositories for disseminating and preserving scholarly and creative work of students, faculty, and staff, usually with leadership from the college library. Liberal arts colleges may be less likely than research universities to host the repository on campus, choosing instead to outsource hosting to profit or not-for-profit services including NITLE's (National Initiative for Technology in Liberal Education) DSpace service, BEPress's Digital Commons, and Longsight.com. Many of these same colleges host online journals, particularly through the Digital Commons service. Journals hosted by liberal arts colleges often focus on publishing student work. Examples include *Constructing the Past*, a publication of the Nu Gamma chapter of Phi Alpha Theta and the Department of History at Illinois Wesleyan University (http://digitalcommons.iwu.edu/constructing); *Macalester Islam Journal* at Macalester College (http://digitalcommons.macalester.edu/islam); *Episteme: Student Philosophy* from Denison University (http://journals .denison.edu/episteme/); and the *Rollins Undergraduate Research Journal* (http://scholarship.rollins.edu/rurj/).

For students, whether writing as coauthors with a professor in a disciplinary journal or as sole authors in a campus-based journal, publication helps to close the loop of inquiry and illuminate the complete cycle of scholarly communication, moving them from engagement with library research through engagement with the primary evidence of their discipline to the experience (both gratifying and risky) of offering original contributions for public viewing and critique.

Author Rights Management and Copyright Education

Liberal arts college libraries often take the lead on their campuses on copyright education for students, faculty, and staff, helping the community to understand both their obligations under copyright and their rights and encouraging authors to manage their rights in a way that meets their scholarly interest in broad dissemination. Illinois Wesleyan University, for instance, covers Creative Commons licensing and the SHERPA RoMEO inventory of publisher policies on open access in its "Copyright Information" resource mounted on LibGuides, and Coates Library at Trinity University provides information on open access, SPARC, and other scholarly communication reform initiatives as part of a guide to faculty on compliance with the university's open-access policy. The Oberlin College Library hosts the well-developed website "Transforming Scholarly Communication," which includes sections on author rights, open access, repositories, and national and international initiatives.[15]

Information Literacy

The focus on the processes of research or scholarly inquiry makes information literacy especially important to the liberal arts curriculum and gives liberal arts college libraries an important opportunity to integrate information literacy instruction with education in the structures and processes of scholarly communication. In its "Information Literacy Competency Standards for Higher Education," the ACRL stipulates that an "information literate student understands many of the economic, legal, and social issues surrounding the use of information," and this can and should include the ways scholarly knowledge is created, evaluated, disseminated, organized, and preserved.[16] A publication program can give this aspect of information literacy more immediate meaning, helping students experience both the satisfaction and the risk of committing original work to the public sphere.

Open Data

Inquiry-centered pedagogy is dependent on the accessibility of primary evidence of many kinds, including qualitative and quantitative data sets in the social and natural sciences. Participation in open-data initiatives has developed more slowly in liberal arts colleges than advocacy for open access to peer-reviewed scholarship, but as the Berlin Declaration on Open Access to Knowledge in the Sciences and Humanities argues, open access should include "original scientific research results, raw data and metadata, source materials, digital representations of pictorial and graphical materials and scholarly multimedia material" in addition to reports of research results, and there will be increasing participation in the liberal arts sector.[17] The research of some liberal arts college faculty, like that of their Research I colleagues, is supported by grants from agencies (e.g., the National Institutes of Health and the National Science Foundation) that already require them to share their research data, and librarians at liberal arts colleges provide guidance on options for compliance.[18] Moreover, some liberal arts colleges are developing their own repositories for sharing data sets created by their faculty or students (for pedagogic or research purposes), including Carleton College and Grinnell College.[19]

Professional Advocacy and Leadership

Librarians at liberal arts colleges have also been active professionally in advocacy of reform of the scholarly communications system. Advocacy of this sort can be expected to grow in importance, with each sector of higher education needing to represent and explain its own interests and needs in public forums while continuing to collaborate on common and mutually reinforcing strategies. Librarians at liberal arts colleges have served as leaders and members of committees like the SPARC Steering Committee and ACRL's Scholarly Communications Committee (first chaired by Ray English of Oberlin College) and have helped educate the profession through regular columns and blogs.[20]

Liberal arts college libraries have also engaged directly in advocacy of specific issues. For example, the Oberlin Group is a signatory to the "Berlin Declaration" and contributed comments to the 2012 White House Office of Science and Technology Policy Request for Information on public access to peer-reviewed scholarly publications resulting from federally funded research.[21]

Scholarly Communication and the Role of the Liberal Arts College Library

BY DIANE J. GRAVES

The conversation on scholarly communication (often referred to as a "crisis") has its origins in the mid-1980s.[22] At that time, the balance of trade between the United States and its trading partners in Europe was so far out of balance that U.S. products could not compete internationally. The Reagan administration, seeking to correct the problem, devalued the dollar at the so-called Plaza Accord on September 22, 1985.[23] In that moment, the price of journals in many STEM fields jumped—in some cases by as much as 25 percent. Many of the top journals were published by British or European for-profit houses, such as Pergamon, Elsevier, Springer,

Wiley, Blackwell's, and Taylor and Francis. The devalued dollar had a huge impact on academic libraries that subscribed to those publishers' products.

Under any other economic model, those journals would have faced the fate of U.S. products in Europe prior to the decision to depreciate the U.S. currency: libraries would simply have refused to purchase them, perhaps seeking cheaper alternatives. But therein lies the challenge faced by libraries that support any kind of scholarly enterprise: each journal is, in its way, its own monopoly. If a particular title is central to the study of a particular field or subfield, the library that supports it must continue to buy it.

To what had to be the delight of the European journal publishers, U.S. college and university libraries begged, scrounged, recalculated budgets, cancelled titles, plundered the monographs budget—and continued many subscriptions. The big European publishers realized that they could indeed charge "what the market would bear," and the market appeared to be limitless for top-tier journals. Prices began the steady climb that haunts us to this day—almost twenty-seven years after the shock of those first price hikes hit academic library budgets.

TOO SMALL TO PLAY?

One of the most puzzling aspects of the entire conversation around scholarly communication—the impact of existing models, the search for alternatives, the need for advocacy—is the assumption that it is the purview of Carnegie Research I institutions first and foremost, followed by those institutions with robust doctoral programs. The corollary is that small academic libraries—college libraries at liberal arts institutions, in particular—are not significant players in the conversation, nor should they be. Many in the academy, including those who work at such institutions, tend to think that the liberal arts college environment is too small to have a significant voice in the debate over alternatives to traditional models. What need is there for small college faculty to understand intellectual property rights or alternatives to copyright and the relationship to access, or even to be terribly concerned over where they might choose to publish?

Similar assumptions and arguments abound: liberal arts college faculty members focus on teaching, not research. Liberal arts colleges do not expect their libraries to support a research agenda, so these questions are not their concern. Liberal arts colleges are too small to have political influence at the national level, and they certainly have no leadership clout. And they are certainly too small, the argument goes, to support any kind of institutional repository. Their small size ensures that there is insufficient output to justify anything of the kind. Incredibly, these views are shared not only by the professoriate at large research institutions but by some faculty members at small colleges.

. . . OR TOO IMPORTANT NOT TO?

In the past decade, there has been a significant and growing awareness and advocacy movement among liberal arts college libraries as the academy struggles with ways to preserve what is good about the current system of sharing and vetting scholarship while maintaining or even expanding access to scholarly output. Chief among those assuming a leadership role are members of the Oberlin Group of libraries.[24] Scenario developers who look ahead to the next decade and beyond would be wise to take seriously the effects the small college library can have on the very lifeblood and purpose of libraries: the collection and dissemination of scholarly content.

When one considers the niche occupied by the Oberlin Group schools, their influence and place in the conversation becomes much clearer. In many ways, the eighty institutions in that group represent the top tier of liberal arts colleges, but by no means do they negate institutions that are smaller or less selective. If anything, they are the leading edge of a force that could significantly affect the ongoing shift to alternatives in access to scholarly content.

TEACHING, RESEARCH, AND SCHOLARLY COMMUNICATION

At many of the Oberlin Group schools, the research agenda is alive and well—and an expectation of the administration. Though teaching is very much a focus at those institutions, there is a concurrent emphasis on— and even a tradition supporting—undergraduate research, particularly in the sciences.[25] Many faculty members at Oberlin Group colleges are successful authors of grants from the National Science Foundation, the National Institutes of Health, the Howard Hughes Medical Institute, and other significant science funding agencies; it is not unusual for grant proposals to include an undergraduate research component, which can be an attractive distinction to funders. Ultimately, faculty members at liberal arts colleges may not expect to produce the research dollars or output that their doctorate-granting counterparts do, but their research is absolutely an expectation of theirs and their institutions.

Further, the teaching emphasis of such institutions lends itself to teaching students engaged in research about the history and economics of scholarly publishing, how copyright and intellectual property laws intersect with the distribution and control of scholarly content, questions of access, and perhaps most obviously questions of social justice.[26] At institutions that emphasize the liberal arts and a broad engagement with big-picture questions about the human condition, what better cross-disciplinary vehicle is there for discussing questions about the public good, the rights of authors and students, equity of access across economic and geographic boundaries, educational opportunity, and fairness?

POLITICAL CLOUT: SMALL BUT POWERFUL

Make no mistake, librarians and their faculty colleagues at liberal arts colleges find journal cancellation projects and access questions no less painful than do their colleagues at larger universities. Lack of access to core and specialized publications has been a chronic problem since the first glimmers of price increases in the mid-1980s. As a consequence, small colleges have worked to create buying consortia that would allow them to meet as well as possible the immediate demands of their faculty and students while depending heavily on resource-sharing arrangements to fill in the blanks. Rather than viewing their counterparts as competitors, small college libraries tend to seek alliances in their peer institutions.

Those alliances are what allow the Oberlin Group schools to become highly visible leaders in terms of advocacy of such efforts as the open-access movement, SPARC, and the Coalition of Open Access Policy Institutions. Further, many of the institutions in the Oberlin Group serve as a significant source of the professoriate, sending a disproportionate number of their graduates on to seek PhDs across the disciplines.[27] A recent study by Diane Saphire at Trinity University confirms this outcome: using data collected by the Higher Education Data Service, she found that "about 7% of students receiving a bachelor's degree from an

Oberlin Group institution go on to receive a PhD. About 2% of students receiving a bachelor's degree from a non-Oberlin Group institution (that has been the origin of at least one PhD in the past ten years) go on to receive a PhD."[28] (Certainly, the focus on undergraduate research contributes to this outcome.) Thus, those institutions and their libraries have an obligation to expose their students to the existing scholarly communications system, its history, traditions, and the practices and legislation that have shaped it. With that comes the obligation to challenge future professors to think about ways to change a system that many agree is broken.

Just as future professors are currently enrolled at small colleges, consider that some members of the current professoriate—teaching, researching, and working at all sizes and types of institutions—received their undergraduate degrees at small liberal arts colleges. When institutions such as Lafayette College in Pennsylvania, Oberlin in Ohio, Rollins in Florida, or Trinity University in Texas occupy a leadership role in the open-access movement (as each has done), it demonstrates to our academic alumni how important the issues surrounding scholarly communication can be across the academy.

The political impact of small colleges can be as surprising as their role as the nursery of the professoriate. Several powerful members of Congress also received their undergraduate degrees at small undergraduate institutions. Texas senator John Cornyn, a coauthor and staunch advocate of the original Federal Research Public Access Act, is an alumnus of Trinity University. He cares about what his alma mater does in the open-access environment, and Trinity certainly cares about his support. Through that relationship there is the potential for influence at the national level.

INSTITUTIONAL REPOSITORIES AT LIBERAL ARTS COLLEGES

The debate continues about the way repositories for peer-reviewed scholarly content should be structured: should they be institutionally based, or is it more appropriate to let scholarly disciplines and their societies gather content for openly accessible dissemination? Many faculty members feel that their scholarly societies are the logical group to collect, index, and disseminate the content of disciplines, pointing to the early days of print publishing as the model. At the same time, much of the work associated with curation, discovery, and dissemination requires knowledge and skills that only librarians can offer, which suggests that even the societies must find repository support at academic institutions.

Also underlying the debate is the question of content output. At small institutions, administrators believe the expense of supporting an institutional repository is cost-prohibitive for the number of contributions the institution's faculty might produce in the course of a year. Yet when one considers the annual expense of the priciest journals, and then considers the potential value of showcasing not only faculty research but also top student work, small journals, and locally held collections, the real value of such a repository becomes clearer. In a time when colleges and universities are finding it more challenging to justify the expense of attendance and the value of teaching and research to the society, finding and funding a vehicle that makes the college's contributions easily findable by potential students, donors, and others obviate the need for a simple, turnkey system that even a small library can use and support.[29]

Meanwhile, the National Institute for Technology in Liberal Education in collaboration with the Council on Library and Information Resources is launching the Anvil project, a venture aimed at supporting humanities publishing in a digital-only environment, relying on Creative Commons licensing to encourage wide dissemination and use through open-access models.[30] Still in the planning stages at this writing, the Anvil project has attracted a stellar advisory board and is gathering information from librarians, scholars, university presses, and administrators about what is lacking in current publishing models, what is needed, and what features are required to ensure success. Small schools with publishing interests, such as Middlebury College, Bryn Mawr College, Amherst College, and Southwestern University, have combined forces with research institutions such as Stanford, Washington University (St. Louis), and the University of Virginia to support and encourage the Anvil project.

LOOKING TO THE FUTURE

As we consider the profession of academic librarianship for the next ten to fifteen years, it is important to think beyond stereotypes and consider hidden opportunities. Collectively, small liberal arts college libraries occupy a niche that holds much greater power than their individual size would indicate. The ability to respond quickly, to build alliances across the faculty and among peer institutions, to construct programs that benefit not only the professoriate but the undergraduate teaching and research missions—all of these traits suggest that small colleges will occupy a growing leadership role in the search for solutions and new models in scholarly communication.

Toward Building an Embedded Academic Library: The Case of Shaping Drexel University Libraries Spaces

BY DANUTA A. NITECKI

The economics of building libraries to meet traditional expectations for a central place for collections and study, appropriately sized to meet the needs of growing campus populations, challenge administrators to question what this iconic campus facility should be. At Drexel University this challenge has been addressed recently through an evolving recognition of the importance of the library as a learning enterprise, with physical space as one venue for embedding the presence of "librariness" into learning environments. Such environments are purposefully built through capital improvements or configured by students themselves not only where teaching formally occurs but also where learners reside and work.

Influenced by changing learning behaviors, high cost of urban real estate and construction, and an expanding student population characterized by serious focus on preparing for the workplace through experiential learning, Drexel is engaged in exploring ways to embed its Libraries' contribution to the academic experience within the university's landscape. In the past five years, library space has been renovated to meet accreditation criteria for a new law school, and another space has been built to explore design ideas that offer students an environment they can configure for their intentional learning activities. As strategies for embedding the Libraries into the campus evolve, envisioning the function of its central facility has also been undertaken and an articulation of its unique function of offering environments for like-minded intense learning is driving its renovation. I describe here these different approaches to conceiving and shaping library as place.

THE SPACE CHALLENGE AND DEFINING FUTURE LIBRARY SPACES

The beginning of the second decade of the twenty-first century witnessed the suspension of many academic construction projects across the country. However, Drexel continued its capital improvement plan by completing renovations and building its Integrated Sciences Building, furnished with movable seating and tables to offer numerous attractive learning environments within classrooms, labs, and open social spaces. In 2010 a comprehensive assessment of library spaces was undertaken by a team of architects and university administrators. The authors of the study established that, for the size of its student population, Drexel was below national standards in providing such spaces by at least 180,000 square feet. With estimated construction costs of $500 per square foot in Philadelphia and established priorities for expanding classrooms, offices, and residential spaces, there was no likelihood of planning a new or much expanded library building in the foreseeable future. The Libraries was not seen as a prominent contributor to the student experience beyond providing crowded study spaces amid shelving and a newly added retail eating outlet within its late night study room.

Through this assessment process, the concept of the Libraries as a learning enterprise was articulated, and a recommendation was well received to design a model of dispersed learning environments with selective links to library resources and services. Common to trends expressed at other academic settings. Drexel had an increased need for spaces to enable social learning behaviors and group work beyond the classroom. In addition, Drexel was increasingly moving from being a commuter school to a more residential campus, though maintaining its traditions of students relying on digital technologies for access to information and working on class assignments. Spaces in residential halls could not keep up with the growth in enrollment, and so these areas could not offer adequate environments for such new communal learning environments. This opportunity was seen as an extension of the study function the library provided.

Although Drexel was the first university to require students to have a personal computer, not all students today prefer to carry their laptops around campus. Expectations for what should be included in a learning environment were changing, though not fully understood. Group work creates more noise than solitary study, and collaborating to design presentations or solve problem sets requires more writing surfaces and computer-enhanced shared cyberspaces. Access to experts in handling information is increasingly sought through electronic venues such as instant messaging and less through questions asked at a stationary reference desk. Consultations offer guidance in structuring research questions and incorporating information into analysis and presentations. These increasingly are conducted in private office spaces or through new technology-based communications channels.

The idea evolved of offering learner-controlled ownership of the configuration of learning environments to meet the need for group or individual study, with selected devices to facilitate communication. Another driver was to explore ways to maximize information experts' time by offering in-person presence to meet intentional learning tasks and to do so where the learners work, rather than expecting them to come to the librarians. The first design ideas for this approach included the design of the Library Learning Terrace and the offer to place a "hub" for librarians to meet in person with learners in places around campus that house classrooms where students already must go.

In 2011, the Library Learning Terrace was built at the base of one of the university's dormitories, located amid the campus residential buildings. This 3,000-square-foot space, with flexible furnishings, is the first response to the well-articulated shortage of library and learning environments concluded the year before. Utilizing furnishings from Herman Miller, it also offers small whiteboards on wheels and an assortment of chairs and tables to seat sixty-seven. One large wall was prepared as an erasable writing surface, for writing and drawing, to organize concepts, develop outlines, evolve formula, visualize designs, or simply communicate playful reactions to life with cartoons or messages. The only stationary furnishings are a security desk at the entrance and a three-part hub where librarians or other tutors or faculty can offer guidance either in the open or with some privacy by enclosing a space by moving a fabric canopy. When not used by experts, these spots are available to students as well. No physical books or computer workstations are placed here, though users bring their own collections through access via wireless networks to the Libraries electronic resources and other Internet data. The purpose of the Terrace is to enable students to develop and exercise intentional learning by taking ownership of such work, becoming self-sufficient in their use of resources but seeking guidance as needed.

An evaluation of this space was conducted in spring 2012. Occupancy data were gathered by the security guard each hour the Terrace was open, augmented by a brief survey of the nearly three thousand students who swiped their university identification card to enter the facility during two quarters of its initial use. The results of the evaluation are that the space is seen as successfully meeting the expectation for offering a desirable place for group study. Occupancy averaged 23 percent over all open hours, which during weeks of the academic quarter were 9 a.m. to 2 a.m. Over a dozen times during the winter quarter, the occupancy peaked above 75 percent, with more than fifty occupying the facility during a given hour's tally of users. Student perception is that the Terrace supports student engagement, group work, practice of communications with other students, and reflection about what they are learning. Satisfaction is moderately high, especially with the facility's sense of safety, comfort, flexibility to create space, and atmosphere, but the small size, crowdedness, noise, and inconsistently performing electric outlets and Internet service are recognized shortcomings. The experiment has been a success in introducing a different type of learning environment, but it also brings attention to the shortage of quiet areas for intentional learning. There are student advocates for building more such facilities on campus, and also those who wish to see more traditional library spaces that offer the variety of quiet and group study among more expert assistance.

With a beautifully renovated top floor of the main library to create the Legal Research Center, financial commitment was made to upgrade the remainder of the W. W. Hagerty Library building. The work involved improvement to the building's mechanical systems but otherwise was planned as a cosmetic reupholstering of the past with new carpeting, paint, and furniture fabrics. Refreshed and more visually appealing, the completed second floor spaces did not respond to changes in learning behaviors, access to information, or the potential contribution of the library to the academic experience or student success. The renovation project was suspended midway for a couple of years while the overall space assessment was conducted and the result of building the Learning Terrace as an alternative learning environment could be evaluated.

Another architect was hired to conduct a series of conversations with faculty, students, and staff to envision the future of this central library facility in order to direct the completion of the renovation in 2012. A total of twenty-three participated in three sessions, during which illustrations of design solutions in libraries as well as office workplaces and retail settings, both in the United States and abroad, were provided to stimulate thinking about the future of the library. Participants were invited to bring their own illustrations of what they wished to see in a library. They were also asked to consider the unique characteristics of this destination in the context of the other spaces designed as libraries around campus.

The architect suggested a few metaphors that resonated well to describe the future learning environments unique to the library. These included conceiving of the facility as having "studios" or places for work, where the work undertaken is learning; offering configurable "vignettes" for users to determine boundaries of spaces for different activities; and simulating a "porch-like" common ground close to individual workspaces for staff who work together but, mostly, independently in offering consultation to clients. Maximizing access to natural light and providing good task lights otherwise, minimizing noise, and simplifying maintenance of surface cleanliness were seen as essential. The strongest shift in emphasis for this space was to ensure greater quiet environments for independent, reflective work while creating a communal atmosphere that welcomed persons of like minds to converge here. Falling short of describing a center for geeks, there clearly is a desire for a learning environment where one can go to do serious learning but also take a break with high likelihood of meeting others there to get such work done. Acknowledging the function of the Terrace, several voiced the ease of placing such islands of social learning anywhere around campus and not requiring the valued resources of libraries to be ever-present there.

Drexel's exploration of library learning environments is at a beginning stage. Continual assessment and shifts in directions are expected. The building of small solutions such as the Library Learning Terrace costs under $1 million and thus can be fairly quickly designed and executed. The investment also encourages change. A Mediascape station for six will be added, and its use in creating collaborative working space will be observed. Such equipment has been adopted by students using the W. W. Hagerty Library without any assistance, except for the addition of a reservation system to allow for groups to plan their work time. Library administrators have shifted their approach to library as place at Drexel from being a space to house books and to place as many seats and tables for study as possible, to being a work environment equipped with access to information, furnishings for learners to arrange to accommodate learning tasks, and intentional offerings of expert guidance and mentoring to support development of self-sufficiency in the work of learning.

Revisiting the Scenarios through Space Planning

BY ROBERT E. DUGAN

The six scenarios in chapter 5 outlining and describing the varying future roles of academic libraries have direct implications for the use and design of physical library space. A key question is, What factors influenced academic libraries to evolve into these roles? Because the scenarios take the reader through the first quarter of this century, a starting place to answer this question is a brief summary of major external changes that have influenced library operations and use of physical space.

The most evident are twentieth-century changes in information technology that are challenging the role of the library as a storehouse of print content. The traditional view of the library is that of a monumental structure, usually the institution's largest academic building, and often geographically situated at the center of the physical campus. It services were based on print information; the library held, organized, and managed information resources so that they could be accessed and available for student use in faculty-led courses and support the faculty's scholarly efforts. But as the ubiquitous availability of computer technologies evolved in the last quarter of the twentieth century, information became increasingly available and accessible in digital forms. By the beginning of the twenty-first century, the library's need and responsibility to house the information's print equivalent as well as to facilitate its access through librarian-mediated services were increasingly challenged.

The second most important change occurred in the institutional mission: the shift of the role of faculty as lecturer to the student as learner as a result of the reframing of the outcomes question from the perspective of higher education stakeholders. The discussion was no longer about the content taught by the faculty; stakeholders wanted to know what students had learned, preferably by identifying and directly measuring the knowledge, skills, and values students had developed from their time and effort while attending college. This was the shift of stakeholder perspective from teaching-centered instruction to student learning.

The synergy of these two changes challenged the academic library as a dominant "place" on campus as well as being the heart of the university. The library's traditional roles appeared to be waning in importance. With the availability of digital information from anywhere on the planet via common computer networks, and faculty and students being able to access information sources with less librarian mediation, library leadership needed to rethink its collection-centric role. Additionally, the shift from teaching to learning would also affect the student's use of the library's traditionally designed study space.

CHANGING STAKEHOLDER EXPECTATIONS OF THE LIBRARY

What are the effects on the institution and its library as outcomes from these two externally influenced changes? The answer to the question recognizes that there was a realization that student use of the library had changed. An early indicator was the decline in circulation counts. For example, a graph from the ARL shows that from 1991 through 2010 the total number of students increased by 32 percent while total circulation declined by 24 percent.[31] Although circulation is an output measure as opposed to an outcome, it is a measure collected by the U.S. Department of Education's National Center for Education Statistics' Academic Library Survey as recently as FY 2010 and often serves as an institutional proxy for use. Some of the decline in usage is attributed to the increased availability of electronic formats of information from outside the library's physical facility over their in-library print counterparts.

A second change involves student learning behaviors. Students increasingly display active learning and collaborative work study behaviors.

This was noted by a shift from individual study to individual and collaborative learning when students increasingly requested the addition of group study spaces over individual spaces. Accompanying this was an increase in social learning, which is displayed by students working together to understand concepts and create knowledge. Simultaneous studying and socializing are common to twenty-first-century college students; they study while using a laptop to monitor their Facebook accounts, text using a cell phone, and share a table to study with friends although none are working on the same course.

The institution expects the academic library to be relevant and to reflect its stated mission. In many instances, this includes a continuation of the traditional view of the library as a place to house collections and librarian-provided services. It also expects the library to confirm its roles supporting students as learners and faculty as teachers and scholars, contributing to student outcomes (e.g., retention and success), partnering with faculty and campus support organizations to identify and measure student learning outcomes, and demonstrating a positive return for the institution's investment in the library.

Students use physical spaces for study and to undertake required course work. Although there are many spaces for students to choose, including living spaces and social places such as cafés, many also expect the library to accommodate their needs as learners. They will use the library if it is designed and configured with their requirements in mind, providing a wide variety of flexible and comfortable learning and social spaces and open hours they find convenient.

Students want learning spaces that range from personal seclusion to group study and from open spaces to cozy nooks. Their mode of study and work may vary within the time they are in the library, such as arriving to study alone and later collaborating with peers to work in groups. Some students request individual study areas that require quiet; others prefer areas that welcome both individual study and an acceptable threshold for conversation. Learning spaces to facilitate peer collaboration include group study rooms equipped with whiteboards, video playback, and projection units for practicing presentations. Students also want areas for teams of two or three with enough table space to spread out print documents and to create multimedia projects while sharing large-screen computer monitors. Students expect to work with a variety of furnishings, from single desks to multiple seat tables, and from comfortable soft chairs and sofas to task chairs (chairs on wheels).

Additionally, students expect their learning space to be integrated with their information and basic human needs. Once they get settled into their space, they want to make sure they will not have to travel far to meet their other needs. For help they want the ability to initiate a virtual chat session or to meet with roving librarians without moving from their learning space. They expect the library also to house areas with food and drink. If a staffed café is not open, they expect the library to at least provide vending machines with the basics for food and drink.

Students have discovered that an information commons, a one-stop physical area with integrated technology and reference help, is worth a visit to the library. This best practice evolved into a learning commons when academic support partners, such as writing and tutoring centers, were colocated into or near the information or learning commons. An intended outcome was to facilitate student learning by providing access to a variety of learning services. As rows of single-user computer workstations were joined by rolling chairs and tables on which groups of students worked on course-required projects, another outcome was the realization of the need for additional collaborative learning spaces.

Students also expect flexible spaces, not just flexible study spaces. They expect the library to provide user-centered spaces that are comfortable—a "third place"—stocked with tables and chairs that facilitate interpersonal conversation for interactive social/group work which, as an outcome, encourages longer library stays.[32] In all instances, students expect the library's furniture and study/social environment, whether they are alone or with peers, to be comfortable in lighting and temperature. They expect a variety of sound level areas to be available, from quiet to conversation (in group study rooms and lounge areas) to mechanical (computer labs and gaming areas). They expect spaces that they can control and configure to meet their learning and social needs. They want movable chairs and tables to allow for different group sizes and configurations. They also expect electrical outlets everywhere to power and recharge the variety of personal devices they carry, from laptops to e-readers to music devices to phones.

Faculty expectations of the library have also changed. As an outcome of the migration of print resources to digital formats, faculty tend to visit the library less often, depending more on access to the Web and authentication through the library to gain access to the full-text resources they need for teaching and research.[33] Depending on the institutional culture, faculty may or may not expect the library staff to assist them directly in funded research efforts such as providing access to literature for writing grant applications, participating as members of research project teams, and establishing and managing institutional repositories. Faculty expect the library directly to support students and their needs to complete course assignments and to help them acquire the necessary information literacy skills to find, retrieve, and analyze information sources by face-to-face librarian mediation, live or recorded library instruction sessions, and other library-created help tools.

The library wants to be relevant to the institution's mission and to add value for its community members. As a result of the changes in perspectives and expectations, libraries are realigning their infrastructure (staff, collections, technology, and facilities) from being library-centered, primarily print information management and services, to supporting student and faculty expectations directly as well as partnering with other campus units supporting teaching, learning, and research. This includes increasing and expanding support of student learning and for student learning outcomes, seeking ways to provide a direct and positive impact on the scholarly work of the faculty, and redesigning its physical space to increase collaborative efforts with the objective of becoming the primary informal learning space on campus.

COMMON WAYS TO RECONFIGURE SPACE

Unless the institution is building a new academic library, redesigning and renovating the current library space to accommodate additional service roles and student learning behaviors are required. The desired outcome is a hub of informal learning on the campus, with flexible space that provides additional and varied study space for students, accommodates campus learning partners such as writing centers, and increases the space allotted for social interactions including lounge areas along with places for in-library food and drink.

In most of the twentieth-century-designed libraries, the print stacks occupy the largest physical footprint in the facility. There is a certain level of tension between the costs of storing little-used print materials in open stacks and the value of bringing in other functionalities such as study space and academic support units including writing centers and information technology help functions. Implementing a variety of ways to relocate or reshelve print materials is often a first-choice solution to decreasing this footprint. The most popular solutions include decreasing the number of volumes in the library by weeding the collection, replacing the common fixed stacks with compact shelving, and relocating print volumes to off-campus remote storage. Each of these three solutions has advantages and disadvantages related to faculty concerns about weeding, the cost of compact shelving versus the amount of space saved, and the accessibility of remotely stored items. A more recent and increasingly popular alternative is the use of automated storage and retrieval systems, which employ robotic technology to store low-use materials on-site, usually in a structure adjacent to the library and specifically built for this storage function.

Another means to reallocate space is by removing specific library functions from the building. This may include relocating backroom functions such as cataloging and print materials processing out of the main library and into institutionally owned or leased space. It may also be possible to disengage a function from the physical space. For example, reference librarians can become rovers, walking throughout the library or visiting students in their learning spaces when their help is requested. Another means to help students and faculty access information is to embed librarians in academic departments, satellite branches, or learning spaces in nonlibrary buildings or dorms.

A more recent alteration of library space is to provide less space for fixed desktop workstations. The information commons as originally designed included enough workstations to have few, if any, wait queues. A reduction in the number of fixed desktop workstations has been made possible by laptops with adequate functionality and size to enable mobility. As stated in the chapter 5 scenarios, the tablet format or smartphone may soon replace laptops.

The space saved through these means may be reallocated to student-requested study and social spaces, but not all saved space may be converted into student space. Collaboration has an increasingly important role—among students, between librarians and students, between librarians and faculty, and between the library and other institutional support units—and face-to-face space for such collaborative efforts requires a physical footprint. The library is becoming an important space for housing and sustaining such partnerships to support student learning and the faculty's teaching and research needs.

THE SIX SCENARIOS AND LIBRARY SPACE

Two questions are relevant to the scenarios in chapter 5: What library space design and usage issues arise from a review of the scenarios? How do the scenarios envision supporting student learning behaviors, partnering with other campus units to support learning activities, and integrating student learning and social needs?

The scenarios are stated from the library's perspective. Whereas the authors of the scenarios identified assumptions, the following review of library space in the scenarios assumes that assessments were conducted to learn what library users and nonusers wanted when considering the current and future use of the library's space. It also assumes that the library aligned its considerations of space design and utility closely with its internal operations plan as well as the with institution's mission, vision, and current strategic plan.

Scenario One: The Present Is the Future

The library retains a traditional commitment to supporting its print and digital collections but tips the balance toward the latter. The library retains its traditional services (circulation, reference, and interlibrary loan). The primary motivation for this scenario is to meet the institutional mission with the expectation of an online environment that supplements traditional campus life. Digital services continue to expand.

Space implications. The space used for, and needed, for print materials probably does not increase with the shift to digital materials, and a likely accompanying systematic weeding project will be needed when shelf space gets too full. Space to accommodate staff probably does not increase or decrease by undertaking this traditional role. Because of this approach, students likely view the library as a place for collections, face-to-face interactions with library staff, and individual studying. Collaborative learning spaces inside the library are scarce, and students may not have access to social spaces. It is unlikely that the library can share its space with other campus learning partners.

Scenario Two: Press a Button Library

This virtual library views its primary role as a mediator for securing and maintaining subscriptions to licensed library resources provided to the institution's community via the Web. Librarians or their service vendors interact with students in the virtual space through mobile communication devices. The primary motivations of the scenario are to provide most library services online and to accommodate a move of classroom learning to the library's facility.

Space implications. The physical footprint needed by the remaining library functions continues to decrease. Even the need for fixed workstations used by students to access the content while in the library decreases because students have their own mobile devices. The library staff is disassociated from the library space and manages licensed content and responds to student information needs using their mobile devices. Space for the library's traditional functions continues to yield to other institutional and academic needs. Students do not associate the library as "place" and likely do not see the library as adding much to their learning activities other than access to electronic content.

Scenario Three: The Library Is a Learning Enterprise

This library is engaged with classroom faculty to teach information and visual literacy competencies, as members of research teams, working collaboratively with learning support services across the campus, and assessing student learning outcomes. The technologically advanced learning activities are present inside the library's space, including inviting instruction space, classrooms, and support services (e.g., writing tutors). Librarians leave the library space to visit students where they are or use videoconferencing for office visits. The primary motivation for this scenario is to position the library as an institutional partner in student learning, recruitment, and retention, as well as to collaborate with faculty on teaching and research.

Space implications. This library may still be collecting content and, unlike scenario two, the librarians are physically associated with institutional space and are working with classroom faculty. Therefore, there are traditional spaces and functions such as collections and service desks. Because in this scenario the library partners with other campus learning support services in addition to providing face-to-face services and content, students view the library as an active learning space. Librarians may be out in the classroom and around campus, but they likely return to offices inside the library. The library probably has several collaborative spaces it uses to work with the faculty on their teaching activities, such as revising courses and reviewing student work, and for working on research grants. As a result of librarians working inside and outside the library, the staff may actually occupy more physical space than in the past because of collaborations in the library, particularly since faculty offices are often not designed to accommodate groups.

Scenario Four: Expanding Service Roles (Especially Those External to the Library)

The library has greatly downsized its physical collections and traditional services by expanding its digital collection and contracting circulation and e-reserve services from a larger, national cooperative. It also outsources services related to collection management and no longer staffs a reference desk. The physical space emphasizes group and individual study space and sharing space with selected campus support units (e.g., the writing center). The library staff has assumed expanded service roles as partners to teaching, learning, and research: they work in a center for digital initiatives; work closely with academic programs to support mutually agreed-on student learning outcomes; and engage in special projects to develop digital guides as finding aids and help guides. With this scenario the library assumes an active, nurturing role of information discovery, supporting and advancing teaching and learning pedagogy and knowledge production for the institution. It is also an active partner in the institutional effort to support research projects irrespective of organizational type or geographic boundaries.

   Space implications. The library spaces for traditional services (print collection and public desks) have been downsized and outsourced. Students meet librarians for scheduled appointments in librarian offices or in collaborative spaces. The realization of a larger digital collection does not require physical stacks space or related staff such as stack managers. In its place, space is allocated for a variety of student learning spaces as well as selected support services including a writing center. The embedded librarians spend more time out of the building than in; they may come to the main library only for occasional face-to-face library meetings.

However, space is allocated in the library to support the conversion of faculty field notes and photographic collections. The same holds true for the conversion of signature collections from the library's special collections. Collaborative space for librarians inside the library is used to support instructional design because departmental space occupied by faculty and graduate assistants is at a premium. Librarians also need collaborative space to work on institutional student learning outcomes. The library houses much of the space used for collaborative faculty activities along with space for librarians assigned to the main library. Because of the number of activities undertaken, the library is expanding its staff. They need places to work or at least share, that is, additional nonstudent space. Students likely see the library as a collaborative learning space but may not recognize it for information resources.

Scenario Five: The Library as the Campus Scholarly Communication Publisher

Incorporating either the first (the library retains a traditional commitment) or third scenario (this library is engaged with faculty to teach information and visual literacy competencies), this library views scholarly communications as part of its core mission and engages in electronic publishing on behalf of academic departments, faculty, and graduate students, creating new business models that encourage cross-institutional cooperation by integrating the university press, institutional repository, coverage of intellectual property rights, and online/print publishing. The primary goal is to make the library more central to the dissemination and preservation of campus scholarship and research by ensuring that the university effectively addresses scholarly communication through publishing while protecting its intellectual assets.

Space implications. Space use is being reengineered as needed to expand scholarly communications, especially as it integrates the university press, institutional repository, intellectual property rights office, and online/print publishing. Although digital technology takes care of much of the throughput, physical space is needed for the staff to manage the many aspects involved in scholarly publishing, such as managing property rights, which may require multiple conference room/meeting spaces. Because this scenario incorporates scenario one or three, the library is not virtual and therefore provides students with space for traditional collections and services.

Scenario Six: The Library as a More Active Research Partner

Building from the fourth (the library expands service roles) and fifth (the library is campus scholarly communication publisher) scenarios, the library becomes an active partner in research, expanding its roles in knowledge creation, scholarly access to information and data, and data curation. Librarians support funded interdisciplinary research projects by applying their expertise in preserving research data and making research findings and data sets widely available and accessible to the research community at large.

Space implications. The librarians serve as members of the research teams. This work may be undertaken in several physical locations; the library's contribution includes expertise concerning data management, which may not require allocating space beyond librarian offices and supportive work areas. Library space for traditional services (print collection and public desks) has been downsized and outsourced in scenario four; space has been allocated for a variety of student learning spaces as well as selected support services including a writing center. This is inconsistent with scenario five, which includes more of the library's traditional role of space allocated for collections and services from scenarios one and three. As a result, students may view this library as supporting collaborating learning spaces but may also feel conflicted by the library's design and use of its space, perceiving both the allocation of the work efforts of librarians and the space itself as focusing on research activities supporting the faculty and graduate students over the learning needs of undergraduate students.

The rethinking and redesign of twenty-first-century academic library space further the efforts libraries are making to improve their capabilities to contribute positively to the mission and culture of the institution. The library can no longer depend on its legacy as a monument in the heart of the campus as the primary draw for students and faculty to enter the structure. It must become a dynamic and flexible place for a myriad of services ranging from traditional collections management to face-to-face librarian support, but it must also directly and visibly support learning, teaching, and research activities, often partnering with other campus units and taking on newer responsibilities such as encouraging the library as the third place and for creating, rather than storing, intellectual assets. To align with stakeholder expectations, library staff must be active listeners and observers, assessing community user needs, behaviors, and accomplishments. For those students and faculty not taking advantage of the library space and its services, the library must effectively increase their awareness of the roles it now undertakes. The performance of the library can then be evaluated in relation to its success in assisting these users to meet their expectations concerning learning and creating knowledge. The roles the library undertakes should define the space; its space should not dictate the roles it assumes.

Concluding Thoughts

This chapter provides additional reflection on academic library scenarios and shows that additional factors, such as space planning, may be added as libraries select their preferred future. Engagement in scholarly communication offers libraries many options as they explore how to insert a campus leadership role in that area into their preferred future. This chapter is not comprehensive in the identification of potentially relevant scenarios, but it reflects the importance of sufficient flexibility for a preferred scenario to become the basis for the library's vision of its institutional role.

A pessimist sees the difficulty in every opportunity;
an optimist sees the opportunity in every difficulty.
—*Winston Churchill*

NOTES

1. This section is licensed under the Creative Commons Attribution-NonCommercial-ShareAlike 3.0 United States License. To view a copy of this license, visit http://creativecommons.org/licenses/by-nc-sa/3.0/us/ or send a letter to Creative Commons, 444 Castro Street, Suite 900, Mountain View, California, 94041, USA.

2. *Newsletter on Serials Pricing Issues* NS 14 (December 3, 1991); see entire issue, www.lib.unc.edu/prices/1991/PRICNS14.HTML.

3. Anthony M. Cummings, Marcia L. Witte, William G. Bowen, Laura O. Lazarus, and Richard H. Ekman, *University Libraries and Scholarly Commu-*

nication (New York: Mellon Foundation, 1992), http://babel.hathitrust .org/cgi/pt?id=mdp.39015026956246. Ann Okerson and James J. O'Donnell, *Scholarly Journals at the Crossroads: A Subversive Proposal for Electronic Publishing* (Washington, DC: Association of Research Libraries, 1995), www.arl.org/bm~doc/subversive.pdf.

4. Paul Ginsparg, "Winners and Losers in the Global Research Village," invited contribution for conference held at UNESCO HQ, Paris, February 19–23, 1996, http://people.ccmr.cornell.edu/~ginsparg/blurb/pg96 unesco.html. Ginsparg also notes that N. David Mermin later described the establishment of these electronic research archives for string theorists as potentially "their greatest contribution to science"; see N. David Mermin, "What's Wrong in Computopia," *Physics Today*, April 1992, 9.

5. *Bryn Mawr Classical Review*, http://bmcr.brynmawr.edu; *Medieval Review*, https://scholarworks.iu.edu/dspace/handle/2022/3631.

6. Charlotte Hess and Elinor Ostrom, eds., *Understanding Knowledge as a Commons: From Theory to Practice* (Cambridge, MA: MIT Press, 2007).

7. Francis Oakley, "The Liberal Arts College: Identity, Variety, Destiny," in *Liberal Arts Colleges in American Higher Education: Challenges and Opportunities.* ACLS Occasional Paper 59 (Washington, DC: American Council of Learned Societies, 2005), 3, www.acls.org/uploadedfiles/publications/ op/59_liberal_arts_colleges.pdf.

8. See Carnegie Foundation for the Advancement of Teaching, "Summary Tables. Undergraduate Instructional Program Classification. Distribution of Institutions and Enrollments by Classification Category," http:// classifications.carnegiefoundation.org/summary/ugrad_prog.php.

9. Robert A. McCaughey, "Scholars and Teachers Revisited: In Continued Defense of College Faculty Who Publish," in *Liberal Arts Colleges in American Higher Education: Challenges and Opportunities*, ACLS occasional Paper No. 59 (American Council of Learned Societies, 2005), 91, www .acls.org/uploadedfiles/publications/op/59_liberal_arts_colleges.pdf.

10. Thomas Cech, "Science at Liberal Arts Colleges: A Better Education?" *Daedalus* 128, no. 1 (Winter 1999), 197; see also National Science Foundation, "Baccalaureate Origins of S&E Doctorate Recipients," www.nsf .gov/statistics/infbrief/nsf08311/.

11. Larry Hardesty and Collette Mak, "Searching for the Holy Grail: A Core Collection for Undergraduate Libraries," *Journal of Academic Librarianship* 19, no. 6 (1994), 362, 370.

12. "Resolution adopted November 18, 2009 by the Oberlin College General Faculty," www.oberlin.edu/library/programs/openaccess/resolution.html. "Trinity University Open Access Policy Statement," www.trinity.edu/org/ senate/Trinity%20University%20Open%20Access%20Policy.pdf; "Rollins Adopts Open Access Policy," http://rollins-olin-library.blogspotcom/2010/

02/rollins-adopts-open-access-policy.html; and the listing of members of the Coalition of Open Access Policy Institutions (COAPI), www.arl.org/sparc/about/COAPI/index.shtml.

13. See "Harvard Faculty of Arts and Sciences Open Access Policy," http://osc.hul.harvard.edu/hfaspolicy.

14. See DeWitt Wallace Library News, http://dwlibrarynews.blogspot.com/2011/10/international-open-access-week-win_24.html.

15 Illinois Wesleyan University "Copyright Information," http://libguides.iwu.edu/content.php?pid=48382&sid=1056350; and see Trinity University, Coates Library, "Open Access Policy for Faculty," http://libguides.trinity.edu/content.php?pid=159183&sid=1347187. Oberlin College Library, "Transforming Scholarly Communication," www.oberlin.edu/library/programs/communication.

16. Association of College and Research Libraries, "Information Literacy Competency Standards for Higher Education" (Chicago: American Library Association, 2000); see Standard Five, www.ala.org/acrl/standards/informationliteracycompetency.

17. See Open Access at the Max Planck Society, "Berlin Declaration," http://oa.mpg.de/berlin-prozess/berliner-erklarung/.

18. For example, "Data Management Services," Grinnell College, www.grinnell.edu/library/services/facstaff/datamgmt.

19. Carleton College, http://arc.irss.unc.edu/dvn/dv/Carleton; and Grinnell College, http://dvn.iq.harvard.edu/dvn/dv/grinnell.

20. See, for instance, Barbara Fister's widely read column "Library Babel Fish," *Inside Higher Education*, www.insidehighered.com/blogs/library-babel-fish.

21. Executive Office of the President, Office of Science and Technology Policy, "Public Access to Scholarly Publications: Public Comment" (Washington, DC: White House), www.whitehouse.gov/administration/eop/ostp/library/publicaccess; Oberlin Group, "Public Access to Peer-Reviewed Scholarly Publications Based on Federally Funded Research," www.oberlingroup.org/node/13034.

22. This section is licensed under the Creative Commons Attribution-NonCommercial-ShareAlike 3.0 United States License. To view a copy of this license, visit http://creativecommons.org/licenses/by-nc-sa/3.0/us/ or send a letter to Creative Commons, 444 Castro Street, Suite 900, Mountain View, California, 94041, USA.

23. "Announcement the Ministers of Finance and Central Bank Governors of France, Germany, Japan, the United Kingdom, and the United States (Plaza Accord)" (1985), University of Toronto G8 Information Centre, www.g8.utoronto.ca/finance/fm850922.htm.

24. To view a list of Oberlin Group members, see www.oberlingroup.org.

25. KerryAnn O'Meara and Alan Bloomgarden, "The Pursuit of Prestige: The Experience of Institutional Striving from a Faculty Perspective," *Journal of the Professoriate* 4, no.1 (2011), 40, http://jotp.icbche.org/2011/4-1 _Omeara_p39.pdf. Robert J. Lemke, "Accounting for the Difference in PhD Creation Rates across Liberal Arts Colleges" (September 15, 2006), 2–3, www.ilr.cornell.edu/cheri/conferences/upload/2006/Lemke.pdf. See also Cech, "Science at Liberal Arts Colleges."

26. Stephanie Davis-Kahl, "Engaging Undergraduates in Scholarly Communication," *College and Research Libraries News*, April 2012, 212.

27. Lynn O'Shaughnessy, "The Colleges Where PhD's Get Their Start," *College Solution*, January 26, 2012, www.thecollegesolution.com/the-colleges -where-phds-get-their-start. John J. Siegfried and Wendy A. Stock, "The Undergraduate Origins of Ph.D. Economists," Working Paper No. 06-W11 (May 2006), www.vanderbilt.edu/econ/wparchive/workpaper/ vu06-w11.pdf.

28. Diane Saphire, personal communication, April 12, 2012.

29. For an example of a successful repository at a small college, see the Digital Commons at Macalester College, http://digitalcommons.macalester.edu.

30. For more information on the Anvil project, see www.nitle.org/help/ anvil.php.

31. Association of Research Libraries, Statistics and Assessment, "Service Trends in ARL Libraries" (Washington, DC: Association of Research Libraries, 2012), www.arl.org/bm~doc/t1_pubser10.xls.

32. Ramon Oldenburg and Dennis Brissett, "The Third Place," *Quantitative Sociology* 5, no. 4 (Winter 1982): 265–84.

33. Roger C. Schonfeld and Ross Housewright, *Faculty Survey 2009: Key Strategic Insights for Libraries, Publishers, and Societies* (New York: ITHAKA, 2010).

FUTURE VIEWS
OF PUBLIC LIBRARIES

If you don't like change, you're going to like irrelevance even less.

—New York Times, *May 15, 2012*

America's public libraries, of which there are slightly more than 9,000 with over 16,000 total facilities, have shown little interest in using scenarios as part of the strategic planning process. More than half of these libraries serve communities with less than 10,000 individuals (literally small-town America).

In 2006, Public Agenda, a nonpartisan public policy research organization, conducted a telephone survey of 1,203 American adults with funding from the Bill and Melinda Gates Foundation. The resulting report, *Long Overdue*, recorded that most respondents gave the public library an A grade in comparison to other public services, and few adults were aware of the tenuous financial picture faced by many public libraries.[1] As the economy worsened in the intervening years, public libraries have had to reduce their budgets—often significantly. *Long Overdue* recommended four areas needing improvement: providing stronger services for teens; helping address illiteracy and poor reading skills among adults; providing access to information about government services; and providing greater access to computers for all.

OCLC conducted a study to determine the motivations and characteristics of those who really support public libraries when a funding-related initiative is placed on the ballot. The resulting report, *From Awareness to Funding*, found that a majority of respondents were unaware of the range of services offered by their local library.[2] Although many claim that they will support the library, in reality fewer people actually vote to support the library. The public library occupies a clear position in people's minds as a provider of practical answers and information. To remain relevant, this library needs to reposition itself. One aspect of this study explored a framework for understanding the intellectual and emotional rewards provided by the public library relative to possible alternative brands, categories, or activities, as shown in figure 7.1. The framework uses two axes to explore these relationships: the x-axis considers the ability to transform or ability to inform, the y-axis the ability to support a practical goal (purpose) or ability to provide an escape from everyday life.

A more recent survey of 1,012 adults in 2011, conducted by the Harris Poll on behalf of the ALA, revealed that Americans value the democratic nature of libraries as places that level the playing field for all by providing materials free of charge. However, less than one-third (31 percent) rank the library at the top of their list of tax-supported services.[3]

Public Library Association Planning Process

The Public Library Association developed a traditional planning process starting in the 1970s. A succession of books, known as the Planning for Results books, have recommended a process for analyzing a situation, setting objectives, making decisions, and evaluating the results.[4]

The strength of the suggested planning process is to gather and analyze data about the community and its residents in order to make better decisions about the range of services provided. Typically a library uses census data for this community analysis, but it is also possible to combine the census data with other data about individuals in a community (often called lifestyle data). The results of the traditional planning process are the maintenance of the status quo, with libraries establish-

Figure 7.1 Emotional and Intellectual Rewards Framework

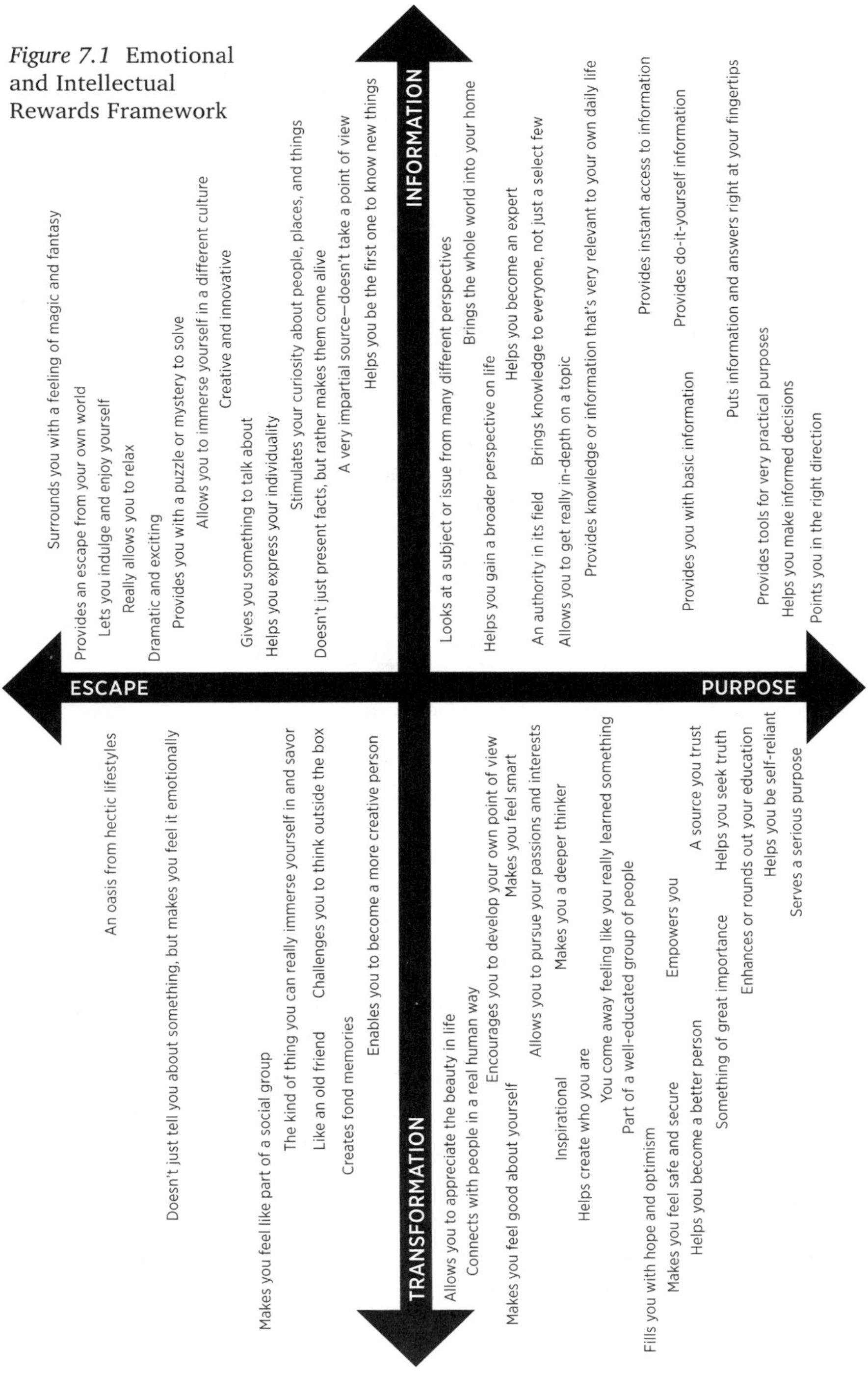
INFORMATION
ESCAPE
PURPOSE
TRANSFORMATION
Surrounds you with a feeling of magic and fantasy
Provides an escape from your own world
Lets you indulge and enjoy yourself
Really allows you to relax
Dramatic and exciting
Provides you with a puzzle or mystery to solve
Allows you to immerse yourself in a different culture
Creative and innovative
Gives you something to talk about
Helps you express your individuality
Stimulates your curiosity about people, places, and things
Doesn't just present facts, but rather makes them come alive
A very impartial source—doesn't take a point of view
Helps you be the first one to know new things
Looks at a subject or issue from many different perspectives
Brings the whole world into your home
Helps you gain a broader perspective on life
Helps you become an expert
An authority in its field
Brings knowledge to everyone, not just a select few
Allows you to get really in-depth on a topic
Provides knowledge or information that's very relevant to your own daily life
Provides instant access to information
Provides do-it-yourself information
Provides you with basic information
Puts information and answers right at your fingertips
Provides tools for very practical purposes
Helps you make informed decisions
Points you in the right direction
An oasis from hectic lifestyles
Doesn't just tell you about something, but makes you feel it emotionally
Makes you feel like part of a social group
The kind of thing you can really immerse yourself in and savor
Like an old friend
Challenges you to think outside the box
Creates fond memories
Enables you to become a more creative person
Allows you to appreciate the beauty in life
Connects with people in a real human way
Encourages you to develop your own point of view
Makes you feel good about yourself
Makes you feel smart
Allows you to pursue your passions and interests
Inspirational
Makes you a deeper thinker
Helps create who you are
You come away feeling like you really learned something
Part of a well-educated group of people
Fills you with hope and optimism
Empowers you
Makes you feel safe and secure
A source you trust
Helps you become a better person
Something of great importance
Helps you seek truth
Enhances or rounds out your education
Helps you be self-reliant
Serves a serious purpose

Source: *From Awareness to Funding: A Study of Library Support in America,* Copyright © 2008 OCLC Online Computer Library Center, Inc. All Rights Reserved. Used with permission.

ing slight incremental improvements over their existing set of services. The Planning for Results books do not suggest identifying or exploring the changes that are occurring in the world around the public library or assessing the impact these changes will likely have on the library. The use of scenarios, unfortunately, is not discussed or considered.

A search of the LIS literature shows numerous references to articles that discuss the use of scenarios when libraries experience budget short-falls. Library managers may construct different scenarios reflecting the possible impact of a budget cut if hours are reduced, staff positions elim-inated, acquisitions budget reduced, branch libraries closed one or more days (or permanently), and so forth. In this situation, the scenarios help inform the funding decision makers and perhaps their communities of the consequences of the budget reductions and how those reductions are made.

Urban libraries have been adapting to the changing environment around them and, as illustrated by the Free Library of Philadelphia, city residents see neighborhood branch libraries as multipurpose commu-nity centers, offering business services, tax assistance, safe havens for children after school, and places where immigrants can learn English.[5] Not surprisingly, as libraries are forced to make cuts in services and hours of operation, demand for public library services is escalating.[6]

Scenarios and Public Libraries

The British *21st Century Libraries* report, commissioned in 2004, sug-gested that the future public library must find the right equilibrium between four key factors (the Four Ps): the *people* for whom the library will serve; the *program* of events, activities, and services; the *partners* with whom the library will develop joint projects and services; and the *place* of the library itself, as illustrated in figure 7.2.[7] After exploring several key drivers of change, the report advised that a variety of sce-narios would likely find a place in a community, then described them. Similarly, the Library and Information Service of Western Australia pre-pared a report that explored a set of scenarios as part of its strategic planning process in the year 2000.[8]

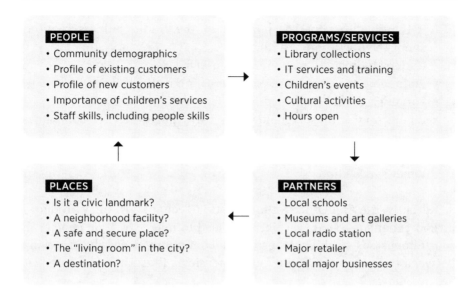

PEOPLE
- Community demographics
- Profile of existing customers
- Profile of new customers
- Importance of children's services
- Staff skills, including people skills

PROGRAMS/SERVICES
- Library collections
- IT services and training
- Children's events
- Cultural activities
- Hours open

PLACES
- Is it a civic landmark?
- A neighborhood facility?
- A safe and secure place?
- The "living room" in the city?
- A destination?

PARTNERS
- Local schools
- Museums and art galleries
- Local radio station
- Major retailer
- Local major businesses

Figure 7.2 The Four Ps Framework

Over the past ten years, the Danish government has mandated that all small cities and towns in Denmark be consolidated into larger units to reduce the administrative overhead. Though the number of Danish public library facilities has remained about the same, the number of library administrative units has been reduced by more than half. As a part of the consolidation effort, the central government mandated that the libraries start to reinvent themselves. The starting point for this reinvention process has been to acknowledge the important trends that have affected libraries and to offer guiding principles about how to make choices about the areas in which to specialize.[9]

The challenge of relevance is leading the public library away from a traditional mindset toward one that is open to transformation and willing to embrace new strategies in delivering meaningful and valuable services. Scott Corwin, Elisabeth Hartley, and Harry Hawkes assert that there are certain imperatives libraries should follow as they move to transformation.[10] Among them are

- Rethinking the operating model or the traditional assumptions about the operation of a library
- Understanding and responding to user needs
- Embracing the concept of continuous innovation
- Forging a digital identity
- Connecting with stakeholders in ways pure Internet companies cannot
- Expanding the metrics that track the level of engagement and customer satisfaction

Recently, the ALA Office for Information Technology Policy produced a report that suggested that libraries need to make strategic choices in four dimensions, each encompassing a continuum of possibilities lying between two extremes. These four dimensions, illustrated in figure 4.1, are as follows:[11]

> **Dimension 1: Physical to Virtual Libraries.** At one end of this continuum is the physical library, often times called the traditional library, with its physical facility and physical materials. As the library starts to move along this continuum it will add a library website. As time progresses, the library will typically provide access to a selected set of electronic resources (the number of eResources will vary depending upon the library's budget). At the other end of this continuum is the purely virtual or digital library. All of the library's patrons have their needs met by interacting with the digital library's website from which they can download magazine or journal articles, download genealogy and census record documents, download e-books, view digitized historical documents and newspapers, participate in online discussions, obtain answers to questions and so forth. From the perspective of the patron, library staff is "invisible" although it is possible to develop relationships over time.

> **Dimension 2: Individual to Community Libraries.** At one extreme end of this dimension lies a library that is solely focused on meeting the needs of each of its patrons, one by one. Library space, furniture, and services are designed to enable the user to

find and interact with library resources in comfort and privacy. The library may offer the use of technologies that are unavailable to most users such as audio and/or video studios with recording/editing equipment, book printing equipment, and so forth. In contrast, community focused libraries provide work and meeting spaces for groups, holding events of community interest, creating and maintaining archives of local records, and artifacts, capturing the oral histories of community members, and organizing exhibits of local interest. The library may offer expensive technologies otherwise not available to community members.

Dimension 3: Collection to Creation Libraries. This dimension juxtaposes the library as its collection as its *raison d'être*—a collection of materials, a place to come to assimilate information, acquire knowledge, enjoy art, and be entertained. The counterpoint is the creation library that focuses on providing the space, equipment, and services that enable the community to create information, knowledge, entertainment, and art. Authors, performers, editors, and others work individually or in a group to create works for personal use or widespread distribution using Internet-based tools and services.

Dimension 4: Portal to Archive Libraries. This last dimension focuses on the ownership of the media and materials being accessed by the library customer. The portal library provides a set of tools that allows the library's customer to access a range of resources that all are owned and hosted by other organizations. The portal library does not require a large centralized facility and so the library can be dispersed to many smaller and more convenient locations.

The archive library lies at the other end of this dimension. The focus of the archive library is to own the materials in its collection and to provide physical and virtual access to these items. Local materials of significance (often donated to the library) are digitized to provide a broader range of access.

The report identifies several themes that help inform the dimensions and associated strategic choices a library may make. These themes include collaboration and consolidation, which means that collections will change in the face of increasing demand for digital materials; digitization of local materials, which will become an increasingly important activity; and personalization of the experiences and the ability to connect using social networks, which means that libraries must reach out to where people are. Preserving and making local resources available are ways for libraries to shift from ownership to providing access via the licensing of materials; however, there are serious budgetary implications that libraries should acknowledge. Librarian competencies will continue to morph and change in the face of the shifting demand for services.

Michael Baldwin looks at how libraries (and society in general) may be affected by futures depicted in the literature of science fiction, which he uses as a forecasting lens since it attempts to provide a valid though imaginative picture of the future. He advances four scenarios:[12]

> **The Singularity** imagines a future in which artificial intelligence is perfected and becomes a conscious, independent entity that may affect society benevolently or malevolently or may ignore people altogether. This scenario spells the demise of the library as we know it.

> **The Super Future** foresees a robust artificial development capability that is used, along with other technologies, for the improvement of the human condition. Not surprisingly, human-maintained libraries are not needed.

> **Dystopia** imagines a future with continuously improving technologies, but this advancing technology is controlled by few. Libraries, though needed, are likely to be outlawed.

> **Muddling Thru** predicts a future in which technology continues to advance to the general benefit of most people, with the wealthy benefiting disproportionately. Libraries likely continue to evolve in this scenario.

Clearly, Baldwin's use of a science fiction lens leads to a fairly pessimistic view of the future.

One public library that has used scenarios as part of its planning process is the Pierce County (Wash.) Library System. With the aid of consultants, the library developed five scenarios that were shared with the community's significant stakeholders during a one-day strategic vision workshop.[13] The participants at the scenario development exercise were more concerned about the library being a connection/connector for people than about warehousing books and other materials. They hoped for a library that was fun, deeply engaged in the community, and a valued partner with other organizations. The participants used the metaphor "community's living room," a vibrant, beautiful, comfortable gathering place, for the library (for more on the Pierce County Library System, see appendix A.)

The Free Library of Philadelphia embarked on the development of a new strategic plan in late 2011 that used four scenarios as part of the process:[14]

> **Brand-New.** Corporate buyouts save libraries in a recessionary economy.
> - Social assistance services deal with a 15 percent unemployment, low literacy, and a sizable immigrant population in Philadelphia.
> - Public school system is in despair with deteriorating infrastructure, teacher walkouts, and 50 percent high school dropout rate.
> - Technology is considered a luxury good, with refurbished/used devices dominating the market and Internet access at home infrequent.

> **Community Refuge.** Libraries harbor communities from watchful eye of "Big Brother."
> - Jobs are readily available in Philadelphia, especially in education and health care industries.
> - Education is government's top priority, and public schools are significantly improved: 70 percent functional literacy rate and 80 percent high school graduation rate.
> - Community ties and pride are strong; residents have taken an active role in revitalizing their neighborhood.

• Technology is viewed as a tool to support education, with focus on basic tech for everyone.

Wired, Wired World. Virtual interaction dominates and hi-tech library websites replace branches.
- Prior to double-dip recession, implementation of *DigiPhilly* elevated the city's digital capabilities.
- Most city services and documents are now virtual and digitized, and a free Wi-Fi network is established.
- People now want everything on-demand and 24/7, and they demand concise, distilled information.
- Education for digital native students is coupled with technology; every child has a tablet PC, and mobile devices facilitate interactive, real-time learning.

Techtopia. Thriving economy and booming energy industry spur high-tech, innovative libraries.
- Philadelphia is a world-class city, specializing in green technologies and innovation.
- Government calls for collaboration and strong partnerships between public schools and libraries, day cares, and other educational organizations.
- Convenient access to technology is widely available, Internet connectivity is ubiquitous, and innovative education techniques coupled with high-tech gadgets engage students both inside and outside the classroom.

The Free Library of Philadelphia then identified eight key success factors:
- Operational efficiency
- Premium service fee option
- Marketing and awareness
- Programming
- Facility design
- Specialized talent
- Partnerships
- Virtual presence and delivery

Out-of-the-Box Thinking

The value of scenario thinking and scenario planning is that they are useful tools for motivating people to challenge the status quo and providing more responsive and valuable services for a library's customers. Asking What if? in a disciplined way allows you to consider the possibilities of tomorrow and then to take action empowered by those provocations and insights. Clearly, public libraries are experiencing new and unforeseen challenges and opportunities. The question then becomes, Is your library ready to act?

At first glance, Adams County, Colorado, northeast of Denver, does not seem a likely place for a revolution in public libraries. Yet, since the arrival of director Pam Sandlian-Smith in late 2007, the Rangeview Library District has embarked on a remarkable journey to transform the public library. In addition to a deep rebranding effort, the Anythink Libraries, the library district has constructed four new "green" innovative buildings, remodeled three others, eliminated fines, embraced merchandising of its collection, replaced Dewey with the "WordThink" classification (BISAC-based) system, provided amenities such as cafés for drinks and snacks, and recast staff roles. Librarians are now "guides" and paraprofessionals and clerks are known as "concierges" and "wranglers." Clearly staff at the Anythink Libraries must be adventurous and willing to embrace change wholeheartedly, as shown in the staff "manifesto" (figure 7.3).

Sandlian-Smith was hired by the library board to create a library system that was very responsive to customer needs. During her job interview she said, "I believe the responsibility of a leader is to shoot for the moon."[15] She has acknowledged that, although libraries have historically concentrated on the organization of knowledge, the Anythink Libraries focus on the interaction between people and information. The goal is to create experiences that surprise, delight, and inspire curiosity. The library dedicates its resources to ideas and people rather than just to books.[16]

Despite a boxy exterior view, the interior of an Anythink library will be visually appealing, with wooden shelves, fireplaces, stunning lighting, a mix of attractive carpeting, and a "perch" (stand-up stations) where staff, guides, or concierges provide roving service. The library

You are not
just an employee,
volunteer or board member.
You do not merely catalog books,
organize periodicals and manage resources.
You are the gateway into the mind of the idea people
who come to our facilities to find or fuel a spark.

Part **WIZARD**
Part **GENIUS**
Part **EXPLORER**

It is your calling to trespass into the unknown and
come back with a concrete piece someone can hold
onto, turn over, and use to fuel their mind and soul.

employed a marketing firm to help with a rebranding effort that resulted in the name Anythink and the "doodle" logo. The library believes in marketing and public relations in an effort to reach deep into the community. In addition, a G.A.S.P. (graphics, ambience, style, and presentation) consultant was brought in to assist in revamping the look and feel of the libraries. An internal group within the library is now responsible for training and morale.

In 2010, the Anythink Libraries was named one of five winners of the National Medal from the Institute of Museum and Library Services and, as well, the library received a John Cotton Dana prize for public relations. With a total collection of just over 100,000 items, a circulation

THE
WIZARD

charismatic

shaman

intuitive

entertaining

value: guide with
wise suggestions

opens people's eyes
to change

turns skeptics
into believers

THE
GENIUS

problem solver

expert

advisor

credible

value: the transfer
of knowledge

instills
self-confidence

replaces inertia
with momentum

THE
EXPLORER

confident

seeker

self-directed

optimistic

value: connecting people
with possibility

celebrates adventure
and discovery

motivates people
to explore

Figure 7.3 Anythink Libraries Staff Manifesto. Reprinted with permission.

that exceeds 1.7 million and almost 1 million visitors demonstrate the popularity of these libraries. In the land of Anythink, everyone would think that almost anything is possible.

The Anythink Libraries have provided a wide variety of resources that will likely be of interest to other libraries. These resources may be found (and downloaded) from the library's website (www.anythinklibraries .org) via the link "anythink tank." In addition, appendix B of this volume provides more details about the process used to transform the Anythink Libraries.

Concluding Thoughts

Public libraries have shown relatively little interest in using scenarios as part of a strategic planning process. Given the enormous positive response to their use among the participants of the Pierce County Library System's strategic vision workshop, and the emerging literature connecting scenarios and scenario planning to public libraries, we believe scenarios are an effective tool to engage stakeholders and excite everyone, including staff, to think beyond immediate problems and respond to the coming challenges.

Librarians will take on new roles, space will be reconfigured to reflect new and broader purposes, and the ongoing digital revolution will birth a new kind of public institution that is no longer bound by bricks and mortar.

—Sue Dremann

NOTES

1. Public Agenda, *Long Overdue: A Fresh Look at Public and Leadership Attitudes about Libraries in the 21st Century* (New York: Public Agenda, 2006), www.publicagenda.org/reports/long-overdue.

2. OCLC, *From Awareness to Funding: A Study of Library Support in America* (Dublin, OH: OCLC, 2008), 4–10, www.oclc.org/reports/funding/fullreport.pdf.

3. American Library Association, *The State of America's Libraries, 2011* (Chicago: American Library Association, 2011).

4. See Vernon Palmour, Marcia Bellassai, and Nancy DeWath, *A Planning Process for Public Libraries* (Chicago: American Library Association, 1980); Charles R. McClure, Amy Owens, Douglas Zweizig, Mary Jo Lynch, and Nancy Van House, *Planning and Role-Setting for Public Libraries: A Manual of Operations and Procedures* (Chicago: American Library Association, 1987); Ethel Himmel and William Wilson, *Planning for Results: A Public Library Transformation Process* (Chicago: American Library Association, 1998); Sandra Nelson, *The New Planning for Results: A Streamlined Approach* (Chicago: American Library Association, 2001); Sandra Nelson, *Strategic Planning for Results* (Chicago: American Library Association, 2008).

5. Pew Charitable Trusts, *The Library in the City: Changing Demands and a Challenging Future* (Philadelphia, PA: Pew Charitable Trusts, 2012), www.pewtrusts.org/uploadedFiles/wwwpewtrustsorg/Reports/Philadelphia_Research_Initiative/Philadelphia-Library-City.pdf.

6. Keith Lance, Linda Hofschire, and Jamie Daisey, *The Impact of the Recession on Public Library Use in Colorado* (Denver: Colorado State Library, Library Research Service, March 2011), www.lrs.org/documents/closer_look/Recession_2011_Closer_Look_Report.pdf.

7. Ken Worpole, *21st Century Libraries: Changing Forms, Changing Futures* (London: Royal Institute of British Architects, 2004), www.buildingfutures.org.uk/assets/downloads/pdffile_31.pdf.

8. Susan Feeney and George Cowcher, *21st Century Public Library Services: The Function and Role of LISWA* (Perth: Library and Information Service of Western Australia, 2000), http://citeseerx.ist.psu.edu/viewdoc/summary?doi=10.1.1.93.1175.

9. Frank Huysmans and Carlien Hillebrink, *Future of the Dutch Public Library: Ten Years On* (The Hague: Netherlands Institute for Social Research, 2008), www.scp.nl/english/dsresource?objectid=21996&type=org.

10. Scott Corwin, Elisabeth Hartley, and Harry Hawkes, "The Library Rebooted," *Strategy+Business* 54 (Spring 2009): 1–12, www.strategy-business.com/media/file/sb54_09108.pdf.

11. Roger Levien, *Confronting the Future: Strategic Visions for the 21st Century Public Library,* Policy Brief No. 4 (Chicago: American Library Association, Office for Information Technology Policy, June 2011).

12. Michael Baldwin, "What Future for Public Libraries?" *Libraries for Democracy*, July 28, 2011, www.librariesfordemocracy.com/?q=node/83.

13. Pierce County Library System, "Building Value in Our Communities: Strategic Vision Workshop Summary" (Tacoma, WA: Pierce County Library System, 2009), www.piercecountylibrary.org/files/library/vision-report.pdf.

14. Free Library of Philadelphia, *Free Library of Tomorrow: Strategic Plan*, draft (September 2011). Reprinted with permission.

15. Norman Oder, "In the Country of Anythink," *Library Journal* 135, no. 19 (November 15, 2010):18–23.

16. Pam Sandlian-Smith, "Managing Innovation: Creating Anythink," *Journal of Library Innovation* 2, no. 1 (2011): 5–7.

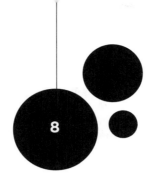

PERSPECTIVES ON TRENDS AND SCENARIOS: PUBLIC LIBRARIES

Preferred Future Planning is not really about the future. It is about folding the future back on the present so that you can make better decisions today.

—*Glen Hiemstra*

We asked some public library leaders to review the set of scenarios detailed in this chapter.[1] The scenarios, which move from "low tech, low touch" to "high tech, high touch," are directed at the "Status Quo" library, the community "Living Room," the "Electronic" library, and the "Happening Place" library (figure 8.1).

The intent of these organizational scenarios is to provide distinct options in which to envision the future of public libraries over the next ten to fifteen years. Each option is derived from speculations about how communities will manage the severe economic pressures they face and how their libraries will embrace technological and other environmental developments. For the most part, the descriptions are nonspecific in order to allow a wide-ranging examination of library prospects. The following assumptions were made in the construction of these options:

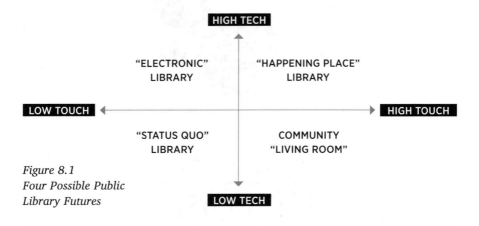

Figure 8.1
Four Possible Public
Library Futures

- Though mid-sized public libraries are the targets of discussion, organizational agility and responsiveness to pressures will be based on size, tradition, scope, and nature of academic programs, governance patterns, and relationships to external systems.
- The view taken for discussion purposes is system-wide and administrative, recognizing that those particular components of the organization and various clientele groups may view the same issue quite differently.
- The time frame is ten to fifteen years to allow the patterns identified to emerge as operating differently.
- All options involve responses to certain basic, assumed conditions: the aftermath of the 2008–2009 economic recession will persist; the library workforce will have to downsize, with library operations reengineered; the pace of technological innovation is likely to continue and even accelerate; the role and responsibilities of libraries will need to change to meet evolving needs and interests of the community; and new performance measures will need to be established to assure accountability.

Though a composite option may be derived from the four choices presented, we think the descriptions illustrate issues and lead to consideration of initiatives needed to achieve a preferred future. Table 8.1 presents more detailed information about each of the scenarios.

Table 8.1

Scenario Characteristics for Public Libraries

TOPICS	"STATUS QUO" SCENARIO	"LIVING ROOM" SCENARIO	"ELECTRONIC LIBRARY" SCENARIO	"HAPPENING PLACE" SCENARIO
Overview	Traditional library building is still used.	More space is provided for merchandising the collection, casual seating, and food/drink allowed.	There is no physical library; use is entirely virtual.	A flexible, dynamic space that encourages social interaction among strangers, collaboration using media and IT, and good quality food/drinks.
Print Collections: Fiction, Nonfiction	Size of collection remains constant.	Size of collection is reduced as books are merchandised.	No print collection; only e-books. Customers can search digitized book collections and borrow e-books, some of which appear as Playaways.	Best sellers only in print form, and e-books are present.
Media Collections	CDs and DVDs gone; all media downloaded.	CDs and DVDs gone; all media downloaded.	Customers can download music and videos for limited periods of use.	Customers can hear music and watch videos. Downloads of music and videos for limited periods of time.
Reference Services	Traditional reference desk is still present and staffed.	Service desks are abandoned and staff rove.	Reference service provided via e-mail, chat, text and instant messaging, and social networks.	Limited reference desk service (staffed by paraprofessionals); professional staff rove and receive referrals from paraprofessionals. Reference service also provided via e-mail, chat, text and instant messaging, and social networks.

TOPICS	"STATUS QUO" SCENARIO	"LIVING ROOM" SCENARIO	"ELECTRONIC LIBRARY" SCENARIO	"HAPPENING PLACE" SCENARIO
Children's Services	Number of programs remains constant.	Number of programs increased.	Videos of children's programs available for viewing 24/7/365.	Programs take place several times a day. Customers are encouraged to present programs.
Staff Para-professional and Professional	Staff remains behind service desks. Fewer librarians as demand for public services continues to decline.	Public service staff are "people persons" who rove the library. Librarians reach out to the community. Circulation and technical service staff are minimal.	More tech-savvy staff to assist remote users—may have other than the traditional MLS degree. Fewer librarians on staff who work remotely.	More tech-savvy staff to provide direct hands-on assistance—may have other than the traditional MLS degree. Fewer librarians who rove the library interacting with people.
Meeting Rooms	Same number as present.	Same number as present.	None	Many such rooms of various sizes with a variety of technologies.
Public Computers	Slight increase in number over what the library now has. A few self-checkout machines.	Moderate increase in number. A few self-checkout machines.	None	Lots of public access computers and rooms for creating/editing music and videos. Lots of self-checkout machines.

TOPICS	"STATUS QUO" SCENARIO	"LIVING ROOM" SCENARIO	"ELECTRONIC LIBRARY" SCENARIO	"HAPPENING PLACE" SCENARIO
Internet/ Wi-Fi	Moderate increase in bandwidth available for Internet access.	Lots of broadband bandwidth for Internet access.	Lots of broadband bandwidth for Internet access; servers to support library applications.	Lots of broadband bandwidth for Internet access; Wi-Fi everywhere.
Collaborative Space: Media	None	None	Computer software available for remote users.	Dedicated area for creating/editing music and videos.
Collaborative Space: IT	None	None	Computer software available for remote users.	Computer software available for use.
Amenities	None	Limited space for coffee and snack food.	None	Good coffee and snack food. Wine bar? Comfortable seating and pleasant ambiance.

Scenario One: The "Status Quo" Library

The library carefully evolves as the familiar and popular cultural institution focusing on the traditional functions of acquiring, housing, organizing, and making available needed information materials including multimedia and digital resources.

The library serves as a community knowledge center and as a place known for expanded use of information and communications technologies. The library has automated most functions and provides online bibliographic access to its collections as well as to most of the nation's published literature. The popular literature collection is rich and plentiful with an emphasis on providing quick access to currently popular reading. Online information services provide for most subjects emphasized by the younger people and the professional communities.

Information services are emphasized, and aggressive outreach programs such as end user searching and information management education are operated. Networks and cooperative arrangements are used extensively to provide backup support and achieve savings in bibliographic control and access to needed materials.

COMMUNITY CONTEXT

The community prides itself as a conservative and tradition-oriented enclave that cares about family values and basic social services. Increasingly, however, the driving forces are economic, namely, declining tax revenues and growing demand for government downsizing. Cost control and cost cutting are prominent concerns. There is a core component of the community that is very active in support of the library. They encourage the library to extend and enhance the information capability of the community through the adoption of practical technological innovation.

Library leaders make an effort to plan comprehensively and strategically, particularly in light of the changing demographics of the community, the new emphasis on telecommunications, and changes in the reading public's interests and behavior.

PHILOSOPHY AND KEY SUCCESS FACTORS

The key question: How can traditional library services best respond to limited public resources and economic pressures in a period of change?

Success of the library is viewed primarily in terms of growth in use of collections, public support for library services, and reputation for responsiveness to individual user interests. The notion of easy access to information resources is promoted, and there is a deliberate library management strategy of focusing on user needs and striving to satisfy those needs.

Experimentation in new services is limited by some lethargy and anxiety among longtime library patrons, particularly in the popular literature arenas, although the public is becoming increasingly enthusiastic about the potential of the Internet. The library provides newer technologically based services as a supplement to traditional library activities.

Scenario Two: The Community "Living Room"

The library continues to focus on physical facilities but evolves as an extension of the family living room, school classroom, and community gathering place. Most service is delivered through a network of small, conveniently located and highly responsive community facilities.

Books are pushed aside for digital learning centers and gaming areas. "Loud rooms" that promote public discourse and group projects are taking over the bookish quiet. There is a multimedia space where kids shoot videos and record music. A central library capability exists to operate certain basic collections support functions, provide document delivery services from the remote storage and central collection, and maintain communication and coordination among local information services and the regional, national, and international agencies relied on for information access and retrieval.

National and regional services provide the infrastructure for local agencies to provide timely, user-tailored information support. Public services are personalized and intense, relying extensively on information technology for access to required information. The staff consists mainly of reader advisors; many of the traditional functions of acquiring and cataloging published literature are achieved through commercial and network services.

COMMUNITY CONTEXT

The community has a young, diverse demographic with families that have, in the past, enjoyed a robust standard of living. The economic downturn has prompted severe cutbacks in all public services including the secondary schools, where libraries have been eliminated with the expectation that the public libraries will fill the gap. There are few community activists who promote the library. Most people support the library but assume it will always be there for their episodic needs and occasional entertainment.

Library leaders make an effort to engage the attention of key leaders in the community but find it is increasingly difficult to demonstrate value added. They are hoping to take on the "school library" role as a response to the economic pressures.

PHILOSOPHY AND KEY SUCCESS FACTORS

The key question: How can library service demonstrate to citizens, commentators, and politicians that they are still relevant and can step up to the challenge of an expanded educational role?

There is a great deal of diversity in the definition of the community's information services, with success of these services tied to intensity of use of library facilities. There are emerging efforts to measure users' perception of responsiveness and relevance. The notion of easy access to information resources is promoted, and there is a deliberate library management strategy of focusing on user needs and striving to satisfy those needs.

Experimentation in new services is encouraged, and special projects receive limited funding to test utility.

Scenario Three: The "Electronic" Library

The library is moving rapidly into the digital age, recognizing the fundamental changes in the way information is made publicly available and the way this information is being used by library patrons. The library now strives to provide virtual and physical access to networked services that deliver information wherever the customer may be.

Since most customers are mobile, the emphasis is on connecting via mobile devices, which are becoming increasingly sophisticated. These users look to blogs, text-messaging services, and networked communities for up-to-date and authoritative information.

The library collaborates with other public libraries on a regional and national basis to outsource many of its functions related to handling services, such as remote storage, virtual reference, digitization, book repair and conservation, cataloging, e-reserves, and records management. The goal is to reduce duplication of efforts and develop increased local expertise and specialization. Space within the library is viewed as a secondary priority, a holding ground for traditional/limited library services and individuals unwilling to or unskilled in taking advantage of networked services.

COMMUNITY CONTEXT

This is a high-density suburban area with a transient population that is technologically sophisticated. There is a readiness to use technology to reduce costs and enhance a mobile existence.

The community hosts several high-tech industries and is seen as a trendsetter for experimenting with technology in the provision of public services. Political leadership looks for ways to achieve highly visible cost savings and avoid potentially divisive public demonstrations of dissatisfaction.

Library leaders recognize that with increasing use of personal computers, document delivery, and data banks, the traditional service role is taken over by the end user and there is an opportunity for the information center staff to serve as brokers among utilities and users.

PHILOSOPHY AND ROLE

The key question: How can libraries grasp the opportunities presented by digitization?

Ready access to information regardless of type, source, location, or format is the key result area targeted by the library. Success will be determined by the achievement of economies of scale as well as by the provision of sophisticated new information capabilities. The notion of remote access to information resources is promoted, and there is a deliberate library management strategy of focusing on the mobility of users. Experimentation in new services is constant and an ongoing part of operations.

Scenario Four: The "Happening Place" Library

Mass collaboration will empower a growing cohort of connected individuals and organizations to redefine social discourse, learning, and access to information. In this setting the library becomes an "Alexandrian" library of all past and present information in all forms as well as a platform for collaboration to unite communities of all stripes in a vast array of information creation and dispersal services.

In effect, the library operates as a coordinator of conversations enabled by network-based technology to create and transmit knowledge. The catalog becomes a two-way conversation and associates the user with any data point that may be relevant to satisfying an information need. This process might start with a conversation between a user and someone working in the library. The catalog might enable users to see comments and ratings of different information and knowledge sources.

The library is viewed as a community repository built by the library and its users collectively. The library operates as a convenient junction where citizens receive instruction, gain access to research materials and state-of-the-art technology, and community space.

The new Web provides a ubiquitous platform for the library to reshape what it means to create information resources and to deliver dynamic new services for a technologically sophisticated community. In effect, the library assures effective seamless access to needed information through an array of services incorporating blogs, wikis, portals, and other social networking methods.

The library facilitates and encourages a culture of participation, drawing on the perspectives and contributions of library staff, technology/business partners, community service organizations, and the political establishment, as well as other public libraries on a regional and national basis.

COMMUNITY CONTEXT

A perfect storm of technology, demographics, and global economics converge for a cultural and social revolution. In this setting, the new Web, an "Internetworked" constellation of technologies, which change user behavior, operates as a robust platform for facilitating and accelerating new creative advancements. People, knowledge, objects, devices, and intelligent agents converge in many-to-many networks that can allow organizations such as libraries to redefine information services.

Intellectual property is shared extensively rather than controlled and restricted. The logic of open-source, open-access, and peer-to-peer sharing comes to dominate the marketplace, with a rich and diverse public domain readily available to all libraries and users. Peer-to-peer sharing of computing power will lead to self-sustaining telecommunications systems that require only the willingness of users to participate and share.

At the local level, immediate cost savings are secured with elimination of most stand-alone library units and their operational staff.

The potential for serving all levels of a diverse community is instantly achieved on a universal scale. The move to the Web 2.0 environment is a dramatic political and economic success.

PHILOSOPHY AND KEY SUCCESS FACTORS

The key question: How can libraries respond to a 24/7 culture and to changing expectations of people who want immediate access to information?

Success of the library is viewed primarily in network usage statistics and the degree to which electronic resources can be easily integrated into the community and citizens' daily lives. The notion of community interaction is promoted, and there is a deliberate library management strategy of focusing on networking as a way of leveraging resources. Experimentation in new services is viewed as a basic measure of success.

Comments on the Scenarios

FRAMING AND GENERAL COMMENTARY

Although the directors tended to maintain that the scenarios nicely summarize four possible futures facing the public library, Siobhan Reardon, for one, observed that the variations among the scenarios should be greater and suggested that for:

- Reference—be bold in the Fourth Scenario and eliminate reference services.
- Children's services—include in one scenario coverage of programs and that programming can be streamed, for instance, to a mobile device.
- Staff—in one scenario present librarians as community connectors who go outside the building to promote literacy and to take information to places such as community centers and community-based organizations.
- Public computers—in one scenario replace computers with wireless gadgets.
- Amenities—insert in one scenario a full-service restaurant that serves as a community anchor.

Larry Nash White noted that, as part of the assumptions for each scenario, there might be a description of the political priorities of each community type and the expected funding needs for implementation of each scenario.

Reardon followed up:

> I would create the community context up front and set the stage for each scenario relative to the nexus point you are using in the low touch/high touch elements. I think what I'm trying to get a handle on here is how you are not offering a single community a variety of scenarios—They seem to be four different scenarios in four different communities.

Greg Buss issues a reminder: "Key future collaborations" likely will be between libraries and other types of institutions, organizations, and communities, and not library to library. He also notes that the segment of the population that can afford to purchase personal devices and rely on mobile technology may use the library less.

Before reviewing the set, several directors issued a reminder: "We gather, organize, and provide public access to the content of our culture." The focus is more on culture than just information.

The participants offered some specific suggestions for clarifying and improving the content of individual scenarios (see below). They also thought that, rather than a single scenario becoming the dominant future, the future was likely to combine elements from several scenarios, depending on the needs of the community.

CHANGES TO SCENARIO TITLES

Not surprisingly, there were some suggestions for renaming the scenarios:

- **Scenario One:** "Doomed to Failure"; "Status Quo, Familiar, or Traditional Library"
- **Scenario Two:** "Learning Space"; "Hanging in There Barely"; "Community Place"
- **Scenario Three:** "Virtual Library"
- **Scenario Four:** "Library as Kitchen: Where You Hang Out, Make Stuff, and Talk"; "Interactive Space"; "Creative Commons" (the

concept of creative interchanges or exchanges); "Creative Place"; "Collaborative Place"; "Hybrid"; "Vibrant" (and the only choice for the future).

PREFERRED SCENARIO

As the proposed renamed titles suggest, the majority of participants thought Scenario Four comes closest to the likely future. However, Pam Sandlian-Smith noted that

> It isn't a matter of preference, but a matter of what is appropriate for one's community. Anythink [see appendix B] is closer to Scenario Two, with some major differences. Our community is a young community and our library service and brand address this directly. We are working on some elements in Scenario Four as we embark on our new initiatives from our latest strategic plan.

Donna Bright added:

> I think most of us deal with finding the balance among the scenarios. Balance between customer demands for traditional services versus customer demand for the other iterations that you have presented. Trying to find the money, making the best decisions with your resources, etc. When I read the scenarios I kept *ticking* off our services as measured against the scenarios and found commonality with all. My preferred? A combination of the "Living Room/Creative Commons" scenario. I see the two as not incompatible. However I'd love to know which company is providing high demand, current downloadable video to libraries.

Charles Pace reacted strongly:

> My preference is really not important; it's what our customers want that matters. Based on our experience here in St Louis, I would say there will likely be a transitional period where we keep elements of Scenario One in place because it is what our

customers expect but over time we will increasingly transition over to a Scenario Four situation. I think that Scenario Three is unlikely at least here in St Louis; social conservatism and inertia will see to that. It's important to remember that just because something is technologically possible, that doesn't mean it will necessarily be widely adopted.

EXTENDING THE SCENARIOS BEYOND FIFTEEN YEARS

The focus here is on important trends and not characteristics of particular scenarios. Many of the participants believe that, given the rapid pace of change, especially technological change, it becomes almost impossible to predict what the future will hold so that planning horizons beyond ten years are unrealistic. Bright suspects that

> buildings will get smaller and fewer. Staff complements will be smaller, libraries will be creating more content, particularly local content, and will take on a higher profile role as archivists for local content. Staff will be out in the community, more frequently embedded in organizations, undertaking training.

Jamie LaRue added:

> Library as publisher: its own stable of writers, its own daily news reporting, *and* a *physical* presence (in the form of community-connected librarians who actively engage outside the building with real people *and* a laboratory for individual and social exploration). Library as a business development partner.

Using a bit of imagination, Jim Fish and James Cooke felt that

- Traditional services and the customers who want them would continue to become fewer and fewer—to the point that they (and the scenario) are no longer relevant.
- Perhaps the "Living Room" scenario becomes the traditional reality of libraries.

- Virtualization is commonplace in all aspects of life.
- New levels of collaboration and sharing [would appear] that we can't even imagine yet.

VALUE OF USING SCENARIOS AS PART OF THE PLANNING PROCESS

A couple of comments portray the scenarios as useful in framing and guiding any discussion of the future. LaRue found that the "the exercise [reviewing the scenarios] mostly reinforced, for me, the *value* of library as place, as one of the assets that tends to be consistently underrated as a personal and public asset." Sandlian-Smith added that scenarios were "very valuable especially when redesigning services, however, equally difficult to accomplish and implement."

Buss could

> see a great value in terms of helping people realize the consequences of their choices. Scenarios 1–3 are all in my mind status quo. Only Scenario 4 is making modest movement towards something new and relevant. What I would encourage you to consider is developing scenarios for Scenario 4. That is where we are now and I would like to have some new ideas and thoughts of how we take that scenario and develop it.

Fish and Cooke responded with:

> Again, they are so helpful in framing and guiding any discussion of the future, whether it be for a general dialogue about the future of libraries, or for a specific strategic planning process. Recently we have had several group discussions with our management staff about the future of libraries and library roles, and we wish we had had these scenarios to frame those discussions. I think the results would have been much more "useful" and "focused."
>
> Given that there are so many uncertainties with regard to the future of libraries, these scenarios really do help people to understand and articulate realities, planning assumptions, and possibilities in a better way.

Annie Norman understands the value of the use of scenarios, with one important caveat:

> My position is that the library profession does not have a well-defined business model. That needs to be in place, understood first, before any sort of strategic planning process is undertaken or is worthwhile. Libraries need to be grounded in our core competencies and how they can be exploited in order for strategic planning to be aligned and effective.

And Reardon responded with:

> In order to be . . . more thoughtful about our future—we really needed to understand our potential exposures, what is trending and how the economy and technology were going to potentially impact our work. Once the scenarios were developed, we used them to test the viability of our objectives against the four scenarios.

COMMENTS ON INDIVIDUAL SCENARIOS

Scenario One: "Status Quo" Library

Fish and Cooke:

> Community context—does this "conservative and tradition-oriented enclave" indicate an older, less diverse demographic? Perhaps worth stating. Another key question—in 10–15 years isn't the question going to be how this traditional library will "survive" in a changing world? Perhaps the question can include something about this, as well about how it will respond to limited resources and economic pressures? Also in this section, won't experimentation be limited by the lethargy and anxiety of some staff, as well as customers? That may be an element worth adding to the mix.

Joan Frye Williams felt that

> the strong suit of this type of library would be reading, not info services. I don't see the professional communities staying with the status quo library. I think the target here is pre-K, families, school-age children, and elders.

LaRue suggested this:

> Add a focus on story times and early/family literacy, which is happening everywhere. Also missing: spell out that "a core component of the community that is very active in support of the library" includes volunteers—the element of civic engagement that is a key response to lost revenue. Also absent is the idea of community partnerships, which seems to me to be happening more frequently even in stodgy libraries. I think . . . that "experimentation in new services is limited" will be true for many. But they can, and will, expand on existing ones.

Sandlian-Smith wanted to reframe this scenario,

> as the public library that doesn't adapt to change, and add that staff are lethargic to make changes. How does this library handle e-content? Your description doesn't say, but I might distinguish between print and digital content. What does the physical facility look like? Is it modern and pleasant, or has it seen better days?

Scenario Two: Community "Living Room"

Sandlian-Smith:

> The way this scenario is framed, it seems like it is being set up at the "bad place." Thinking about the Chicago Public Library YouMedia project (we are now apart of this IMLS project), they

are reframing and owning learning spaces. I see this as a powerful extension and adaptation of the library role. I don't agree
with the connection to "school library" role, which conjures up
another very negative image and is fraught with problems. If
I were writing this, I would frame it much more optimistically
and positively. Not sure that the community wouldn't see the
added value.

LaRue:

I like the content creation piece, but there's some missing stuff
in this role. If community gathering place is a focus, then again
emphasize the development of volunteerism and community
partnerships. Key to this role is space: performance space, public meeting space, small group study space, even conference
space, but probably fewer permanent walls. With the young
families you pose here, children's programming will be huge—
storytimes, reading programs, crafts, plays, etc. I also question
the notion that taking on "school library" is probable. There's
such a profound philosophic difference between curricular support and free reading, and in the orientation of school versus
public library staff. I just don't think that this shift is likely, particularly with strained resources. As far as appealing to civic/
municipal leaders, this is a "library as place" model, right? So
community gathering place is an anchor—and that's the case
that appeals to civic leaders. It seems like you have deliberately
constrained this model to fail. It doesn't have to.

Fish and Cooke:

Community context—why a "very young" diverse demographic? Wouldn't it be more varied than that . . . including
older people? Also, in this section, the sentence about people supporting the library (at least in theory!) and assuming it
will always be there for their occasional needs/entertainment

is important in getting folks to think about how many people really do use/value the library.

Williams:

> [Community facilities would] most likely be shared with other public or nonprofit organizations/functions—more of a multipurpose community center than stand-alone library. . . . the draw for this scenario is the focus on academic success and efficient inventory management + self-service.

Scenario Three: "Electronic" Library

Fish and Cooke:

> The key question is does "digitization" really encompass all you want to ask in this question? How about "how can libraries grasp and/or maximize opportunities presented by virtualization and the mobility of users?"

Sandlian-Smith asked,

> since this is the "digital library," why isn't there training included? In my mind, sophisticated training in communication and production might fit with this scenario.

Williams:

> More likely, the library would serve as authenticating agent for commercial data services, paying on an as-used basis. The same model is currently used in academic libraries—we arrange access and vouch for you, and you download what you need from the supplier.

Scenario Four: "Happening Place" Library

LaRue notes:

> Libraries—right now and in any conceivable future—are community assets that connect not just people and ideas, not just people and stories, but people and people. That's true in all the scenarios.

Fish and Cooke:

> The key question is, could the question indicate that in this scenario the library is fully integrated into a culture that is participative, collaborative, or co-creative?

Williams, noting the question about how can libraries respond to a 24/7 culture, commented,

> I think this is a better question for Scenario Three. The question here is how libraries can move beyond controlling information-based transactions to encouraging facilitating information-fuelled transformations. Our role is to support new ideas and creativity in real time, not just to archive the finished work.

Concluding Thoughts

The four scenarios introduced in this chapter, elaborated in table 8.1 and commented on by our panel of library directors, provide a foundation for constructing a preferred scenario tailored to the community served. A wide set of stakeholders should be engaged in a review of the chosen scenario. Perhaps more important, the set of scenarios should provoke useful discussions about possible futures. Still, as consultant Larry Nash White pointed out, "Libraries need to understand that they will occasionally need to revise their strategic responses; not just pick one and stay with it for ten to fifteen years." Clearly, libraries will construct their own scenarios and revisit them on an ongoing basis, making changes as needed.

Learn the past, watch the present, and create the future.

—*Jesse Conrad*

NOTE

1. Participants: Donna Bright, director of the Ajax (Ontario, Canada) Public Library; Greg Buss, director of the Richmond (British Columbia, Canada) Public Library; Jim Fish, director, and James Cooke, planning and projects manager, of the Baltimore County Public Library; Jamie LaRue, director of the Douglas County (Colorado) Libraries; Annie Norman, Delaware state librarian; Charles Pace, director of the St. Louis County Library; Siobhan Reardon, director of the Free Library of Philadelphia; Pam Sandlian-Smith, director of Anythink Libraries (Adams County, Colorado); Larry Nash White, educator and consultant; and Joan Frye Williams, consultant.

PREPARING FOR THE FUTURE: SOME FINAL THOUGHTS

The future is already here—it's just not evenly distributed.

—William Gibson

As the **"2012 State of America's Libraries" reports, the current** situation appears bleak for many academic and public libraries. "As academic librarians and their colleagues in higher education," we are reminded, "continued to navigate the 'new normal,' characterized by stagnating budgets, unsustainable costs, increased student enrollment, and reduced staff, the pressure on higher education to demonstrate value . . . [takes] on new urgency and importance." As for public libraries, they "continue to be battered by a national economy whose recovery from the Great Recession is proving to be sluggish at best."[1] In such a climate, some may think it inappropriate and a waste of time and resources to ponder the future. Still, we remind those absorbed in the present that now is the time to rethink assumptions and move in bold directions. Leaders need a vision that energizes the organization and its stakeholders as they show others the potential of the library in fulfilling its community role. Libraries, like other organizations, are changing. The scenarios highlighted in this book underscore that change is already reshaping the library—whether academic or public library.

Many changes that managers introduce will likely reflect the influence of new technologies, social media, handheld computer access, new information-seeking patterns and customer preferences, and increased competition for information provision. There will be more reliance on touchscreen interfaces (or those that do not actually require someone to touch a screen) and alternatives to the keyboard. The public will become more visually focused for its information and communication and more reliant on videos from, for instance, YouTube; on social games; on interactive interfaces; and on voice-to-text technology. Through the application of apps and drag-and-drop functions, the interfaces will make it easier to bring up and combine images, videos, music, and other media.

Libraries affiliated with research universities and other academic institutions are collaborating more with departments and forming partnerships to manage (steward) a broad array of digital resources (various artifacts and data sets). As Richard E. Luce explains, the challenge for these libraries is to ensure "the quality, integrity, and curation of digital research information"; sustain "today's evolving digital service environments"; bridge and connect "different worlds, disciplines, and paradigms for knowing and understanding; and preserve research data in a data world."[2] They will also engage more in open-access publishing and challenge the traditional role of monograph and journal publishers.

Although such changes will occur, it is important to recognize that there will likely be increased accountability and focus on effectiveness and economic efficiency. Most academic and public libraries, on an ongoing basis, may conduct studies of the return on investment for their customers, communities served, and institutions or broader organizations.[3] They may also display a calculator, known for its validity and reliability, on their home pages so that others can determine their own return on investment, perhaps the percentage of tuition dollars recouped from library use.[4]

Library directors also expect continued evolution of the professional staff skill set. Further, as Stanley Wilder, who has been studying the demographics of academic librarians for more than a decade, notes, academic librarians tend to be older than other types of librarians.[5] With the unfolding of the second decade of the twenty-first century, the average age of students in master's degree programs in library and information science continues to go downward, but many of these students are not interested in academic librarianship. Recruitment in academic librarianship may remain a problem unless libraries continue to expand the desired skill set of the professional workforce and include individuals from allied disciplines as part of that workforce and charge them with new roles and responsibilities.

Leadership

The preferred scenario from chapters 5 and 8, combined with elements from the other scenarios, the depictions in chapters 6 and 7, and whatever else the senior management team wants to add, can form an excellent vision statement highlighting the service role the library strives to achieve. That vision and the organizational mission statements become beginning points around which to build a compass, as described in chapter 1. That compass summarizes the strategic plan, keeps the organization and interested stakeholders informed of the direction the library is headed, and relies on metrics to accomplish that plan.

Accomplishment of that compass and vision depends on an element that is receiving increased attention in professional literatures: leadership. *Leadership* is one of those words for which there are numerous definitions, none of which, however, has become a standard. In this chapter, we view leadership as the ability to develop a vision of the organization, get others to support that vision, implement the vision in organizational (or institutional) terms, and ensure that things happen according to a strategic plan.

The definition, however, focuses on library directors and the senior management team that helps to shape the vision, as well as institutional and broader organizational leaders (e.g., provosts, chancellors, and members of city and county government). Leadership also applies at the team or group level as members help to achieve those priorities and goals. Individuals might, therefore, be both followers and leaders, and such movement from one position to the other should be encouraged. Clearly, leadership at all levels of the organization will be required to gain buy-in to the vision and to implement that vision successfully. This suggests that, as libraries develop their preferred scenario, they need to consider its implementation.

CHANGING THE ORGANIZATIONAL CULTURE

As library leaders consider the future and what the entire enterprise will look like, there will be increased need to repurpose staff to perform new roles and responsibilities. We have all heard of libraries that have outsourced technical services and shifted staff to public service; repurposing, however, is more than merely outsourcing and moving staff around. It involves an identification of new skills, abilities, and knowledge along with succession planning to include those expectations. An example is the chapter 5 fourth scenario, with embedded librarians. Such individuals are more than subject specialists converted to a twenty-first-century setting. Embedded librarians will have more than subject (collection) knowledge; many of them, for instance, might come with a background in education and be knowledgeable about learning pedagogy, or they might be engaged in curation of data sets emanating from federal grants.

To meet the standards set by institutional and program accreditation organizations, academic libraries may want to combine information and visual literacy, and perhaps other forms of literacy as they play a role in student lerning outcomes at the program and institutional levels. A likely result might be some form of embedded librarians in the preferred scenario, whereby librarians partner with departments and researchers engaged, for instance, in federally funded research projects and play a key role in the preservation of the research, including data sets, and instruct faculty and students in data management and curation.

Staff Abilities for the Present and Future

Previous chapters have suggested some of the abilities and skills librarians of today and tomorrow need. To that list, we would add the ability to solve problems and apply both evaluation and assessment (adaptive leadership); to engage in evidence-based decision making; to think critically; to teach and advance learning in multicultural settings; to engage in multitasking; to be people-centered, innovative, and entrepreneurial; to communicate in oral and written form with impact; and to be flexible (willing and able to assume new roles and responsibilities).

It may be that more academic librarians will come from the archives profession and have backgrounds in instructional design, which is useful for repurposing facilities. One of the better descriptions of an instructional design librarian is one who is "enthusiastic, flexible, energetic, service-oriented, and innovative" and who

> supports student learning by working in partnership with library and teaching faculty to apply learning theories and technology to develop, implement, and maintain general and course-specific online learning objects, instructional modules, and other library instruction materials; facilitates the integration and use of these materials in course management systems and other online environments; and ensures compliance with ADA guidelines and higher education accreditation standards. The librarian assists in the identification of the information needs of on-campus and distance students and in the assessment of the effectiveness of online learning objects and other library instructional materials in improving student learning outcomes. The successful candidate coordinates the library's social media presence; explores new technologies related to online teaching and learning; and trains librarians and staff in the use of new technologies.[6]

In part, however, such a position overlaps with that of an assessment librarian, who is responsible for developing and implementing a structure and process for an ongoing evaluation and assessment of library services and seeing that the evidence gathered is used for accountability and service improvement.

Currents in Scenario Development

The purpose of scenarios is to help one think about the future and be aware of critical trends that will impinge on libraries. These following developments suggest such trends:[7]

- Digital Public Library of America (http://dp.la) encourages organizations to go beyond individual digitization projects to create a shared resource. Through this site, a range of organizations, including the Library of Congress, have made books, images, historical records, and audiovisual materials available to anyone with Internet access. Many universities and public libraries, among other types of organizations, have digitized materials that could be linked to this project. The goal is to provide a distributed system that aggregates collections from research libraries and institutions, not a single database. It should be noted, however, that the Digital Public Library of America will require a fair amount of information technology infrastructure, a powerful and yet easy-to-use user interface, and associated talented personnel to manage the large and complex project.

- HathiTrust (www.hathitrust.org), one of the partners of the Digital Public Library of America, is an international partnership of major research institutions and libraries to preserve the cultural record and make it accessible for the future.
- The Google Book Search settlement will shape the extent to which a vast amount of copyrighted works will be publicly available.
- Public Library of Science (www.plos.org), a nonprofit advocacy organization, publishes high-quality journals in the physical and medical sciences that are freely available.
- Acting as a publisher, Amazon.com provides the means for people to self-publish and make their content available on Amazon.com and other channels, perhaps in e-book format.
- Consortia such as OhioLINK provide their members access to books, articles, databases, and other resources. As such consortia expand they might enable member libraries to manage collections of trade publications and university press publications cooperatively. Member libraries might retain fewer print copies and share the print or digital copy, depending on the preference or need of the user.

Such examples tend to support open access, which is intended to provide free immediate access to, and unrestricted reuse of, original works of all types. Anyone may copy, distribute, or reuse open-access literature as long as the author and original source are properly cited. Scenario planners cannot afford to ignore the implications of more resources entering open-access enterprises, even in the next fifteen years.

If we factor into the chapter 5 set of scenarios libraries serving liberal arts institutions (see chapter 6), new elements will be inserted, making any scenario more complex than we can illustrate in this book. Such libraries, for instance, want to provide students a rich educational experience, one that exposes them to unique materials (e.g., print in archival and special collections). There might still be programs and courses that cover the history of the book, book arts, and the creative uses of the book. For this reason, a preferred scenario might, in fact, address more print material than those presented in chapter 5 do. As well, as libraries invest in commons—be they information, learning, or academic commons—they will have to give further thought to the use of existing spaces and how they want to engage in teaching and learning. Library spaces conducive to, and supportive of, a variety of study and work habits might be considered in a scenario.

Privatizing Libraries

As librarians and others review the scenarios presented in this book and forge one most appropriate to the local situation, it is possible that some communities will consider privatization. When doing so, they should read and reflect on ALA Editions' *Privatizing Libraries*, which asks local officials to answer four critical questions:[8]

1. Can a private company maintain the level of public trust that has been earned by the local library?

2. Will the library director always make the operational decisions that are in the best interest of the community, even if those decisions reduce or do not contribute to the private company's profit?

3. Does the relationship between a public library and its community change when a library is privatized?

4. Does the role of the library as a public good change when the library is privatized?

The preferred scenario influences the answer to the fourth question, especially as it embraces a broader array of services aimed at making the public library more of a community center. An important component of *Privatizing Libraries* is five case studies and collective write-ups, which suggest that the emerging picture is not uniform. Clearly the focus is on how the library became privatized and how well privatization works now. The present volume really adds two related questions: how will the role of the library change over time, and what will that role be? The answer to these questions encourages communities to think about more than a list of present-day services and be more proactive in developing the library's role in an ever-changing, competitive environment. What will the privatized library look like fifteen years, or longer, from now?

Libraries Merely Trying to Keep Up

When developing and testing the scenarios on different library directors, we encountered some libraries that have encountered severe budget cuts on an ongoing basis and, as a result, were forced to lay off staff. The size of the staff might now be reduced to anywhere from five to thirteen professional staff members. The changed fiscal climate may not be directly linked to the economic recession and recovery; in fact, that climate might actually predate 2008. To make matters worse, there is likely to be no opportunity to alter the situation in the foreseeable future, and the community served may not want the library to eliminate or realign any of the services provided. The library is probably setting priorities and aligning its resources with community partners; focusing on services that are high priority, effective, and innovative; and aligning library spaces to support group and individual learning. Clearly, the word *alignment* is becoming more popular as everyone working in the library assumes additional work roles and duties, and the library may be reducing the number of hours it is open to the public. Since the challenge is to confront the situation and engage in realignment, the library leadership should not forgot to ask:

- To what extent does a focus on the present prevent the library from creating and working toward a vision such as one represented in the scenarios?

- To what extent can the present and the future be viewed together?
- Is the future a prisoner of the present?

Revisiting Space Planning

Traditionally, libraries have needed additional space to manage growing print collections, and librarians have hoped that shelving needs would not drive library space design. As Scott Bennett explains, "This hope builds on the promise of using virtual space to reduce the demand for physical space." As we get further into the twenty-first century, there is greater emphasis on both physical and virtual space and a realization that learning spaces across a campus are often in need of redesign to accommodate how students learn and how professors best advance learning. Bennett continues, "The challenge in investing in non-classroom space is to focus on the specific learning behaviors the institution wants to foster." He asks librarians to look at libraries from the perspective of "information consumers" and to view the pressing question as "Should . . . [the] main campus library continue to serve only about a third of the institution's students with any frequency? Or should it adopt a strategy that moves the library closer to the needs of the remaining two-thirds of the college's students. And is this an either/or choice for the library, or a both/and choice?"[9] Bennett sees students as learners and favors library space design to be primarily concerned with learning. Apparently services for them should be directed at fostering learning.

Among the many questions Bennett raises, these stand out as libraries review the various scenarios and construct the one most meaningful to their managerial leaders:

What impact(s) does the library wish to have on student learning? What impact does it now have?

For what reasons and how frequently do we want students to be in the library building? How do our aspirations for student use compare to their actual use of the library building?[10]

To address these questions partially, academic libraries are investing more in learning or academic commons as they seek to expand their social and educational roles. Undoubtedly such commons will continue to evolve, but libraries will see them as one venue for attracting and serving faculty and students. In addition, there will likely be more collaborative study spaces, study or learning rooms with a full complement of information technologies and movable furniture to accommodate group learning. More libraries will apply ethnographic tools and techniques to understand the information-seeking behavior, information use patterns, and learning and communication styles of students. That understanding will lead to more refinements in facilities.[11]

Libraries may experiment with products such as Microsoft Surface, a commercial computing platform that enables people to share digital content as the system recognizes physical objects, such as cell phones, and allows hands-on, direct control of content such as photos, music, and maps. The Surface turns an ordinary tabletop into a dynamic surface that provides interaction with all forms of digital content. Clearly, user-centered design will drive the construction and remodeling of physical space and the virtual library. As well, library spaces must be flexible and accommodate various information needs and expectations.

Issues of Importance to the Broader Organization

As library directors and their senior management team settle on the skill set, abilities, and knowledge areas for the future workforce and build those expectations into their succession planning, they must also identify those issues important to the broader organization as it seeks to meet the increased demands of stakeholders. One of demands relates to accountability and how the library adds to its parent body's ability to prove its effectiveness, high quality, and value while maintaining a high level of customer satisfaction. For example, institutions of higher education are likely to create a simple scorecard or dashboard that enables families and others to track and report how the college or university stacks up against its competitors on graduation rates, time-to-degree rates, retention rates, what a degree actually costs students, and how much debt a student can expect to incur by the time of graduation. For-profit institutions already report to the federal government on issues of affordability and value, in terms of student earnings and debt. Academic libraries, as well as other support units, will assume new roles and need management information systems to gather and report such data. Any preferred scenario must ground the library in the context of the broader organization and its future orientation.

SCENARIOS IN THE BROAD UNIVERSITY SETTING

Libraries serving campuses with a presence, either physical or virtual, in other countries need to ensure that their preferred scenario applies internationally. It seems that many universities embrace a planning process that might be called a simple extrapolated future with today's trends continuing (ignoring other factors already at work). However, there are scenarios that apply at the institutional level, and these do not specifically mention the role of libraries and other support services. It may be that librarians want to place their preferred scenario in an institutional context, especially if there is a set of institutional scenarios.

Swinburne University of Technology in Australia used scenarios to explore the future of the university. That study envisioned six drivers of change, assessed in terms of opposing end states, within which various outcomes can be explored:[12]

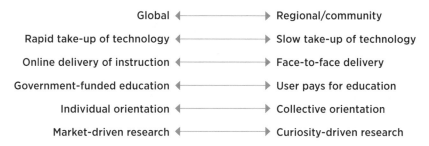

A factor that has a global impact on institutions of higher education is the competition for students and faculty. The goal is to increase the revenue stream coming into institutions.

James Duderstadt suggested that, with the rapid pace of change in all sectors, universities of the future might be unrecognizable. He postulated nine scenarios, including these two:[13]

> **Cyberspace University,** which is linked to an information network providing services when and where needed. The classroom experience disappears and is replaced by the anywhere, anytime online experience. Totally distance education institutions require much less physical space.

Lifelong University, which is committed to a lifetime of interaction with its students. It seeks the active participation of alumni as teachers, advisors, and role models (and occasionally as students).

In 2003 the OECD developed several scenarios that might be used to stimulate thinking about the future of higher education. Among those scenarios is one called "Diversity of Recognized Learning," in which the formal system of higher education disappears as technology is used as an enabler for the diffusion of information and knowledge. People learn in different ways and there is an open-source model for education.[14]

The Futures Project at Brown University developed seven scenarios to serve as discussion tools about possible futures in higher education. Among them are these two:[15]

New providers help build a skilled workforce. Community colleges and some universities are aggressively pursuing partnerships with selected employers to develop certification courses that are necessary in the marketplace.

In search of the new economy. Private companies and branches of existing universities have had an impact when they are allowed to compete with existing universities in other countries.

Stéphan Vincent-Lancrin suggested six scenarios that one or more universities in a country might pursue. Two merit mention:[16]

Embrace-change scenario, which aggressively pursues private funding to compensate for public funding.

Market-led scenario, in which universities concentrate on specialized niches, where they can be market leaders by embracing productivity-enhancing information technology for teaching, and the outsourcing of publicly funded science.

In 2006 the OECD developed four new scenarios to provoke discussion. There is some overlap with the previously identified OECD scenarios:[17]

Open Networking. Higher education is internationalized and is based more on collaboration than on competition (harmonized higher education systems). Students design their own curriculum and degrees and choose their courses from the global education network. Courses are delivered online and students interact intensively with fellow students, instructors, and experts in industry. International networks are facilitated by lower costs of communication and by information and communications technology.

Serving Local Communities. A majority of universities are focused on addressing national, regional, and local economic and community needs in their teaching and research. These universities are mainly publicly funded and administered. A small number of elite universities continue their focus on research and work to maintain their position in top international rankings. This scenario is a response to the growing antiglobalization movement based on economic and cultural grounds.

New Public Management. When publicly funded, universities are responsive to market forces and financial incentives. Boundaries between public and private higher education institutions blur as universities rely more on tuition, business, and private foundation donations to ease the funding gap. There is national competition for public research funding. Students and their families are interested in the quality of teaching (learning), and employability is a real concern in making decisions about which university to attend.

Higher Education Inc. Higher education institutions compete globally to provide education services and research services on a commercial basis. Research and teaching are increasingly disconnected. In addition to fierce competition for financial resources, institutions compete for the best students and faculty. There is increased mobility of students and cross-border higher education. This results in some universities developing international reputations for high-quality undergraduate education while others specialize in graduate (and postgraduate) education.

The University of California, despite its historical strengths and contributions, found itself at a crossroads in 2006. The UC leaders felt that its reputation for excellence, its place on the cutting edge of knowledge and creativity, and its relevance to the pressing needs of California were at stake. Thus, its Long-Range Guidance Team explored four scenarios as part of a planning process to define an overarching vision and strategies both for today and the year 2025:[18]

Beyond the Tipping Point. In this worst-case scenario, budget and demographic pressures take such a toll that talent flees, prestige declines, and sharply reduced research funding make it difficult to attract and retain talent.

Virtuous Circle. In this best-case scenario, California's economic engine is restored and fuels higher levels of economic prosperity. The State decides to raise its financial support for the UC system of ten campuses. The increased funding leads to energy self-sufficiency for each campus and breakthroughs in health care.

UC Polytechnic. Given higher funding for K–12 schools, the performance gap is reduced so that more high school graduates become eligible for admission to one of the UC campuses. This flood of undergraduate students forces cuts in graduate education and research. Other universities from around the world rush to fill the research vacuum.

Complementary Campuses. While State funding continues to decline, each UC campus specializes in what it does best (and stops trying to be all things to all people). Each campus boasts at least one center of excellence in research.

The report concludes that there is a need for a renewed social contract with the State of California (not likely given the state's worsening budget deficits) and that each campus must develop unique profiles of complementary strength and increase graduate enrollment to maintain the UC's research-intensive nature.

In 2007 the Universiti Sains Malaysia involved campus administrators, faculty, and other interested stakeholders in an extensive project to consider future higher education scenarios. This project resulted in the selection and exploration of five scenarios. The students and the university staff agreed on two as their preferred options: À la Carte University, which educates students on an international basis and meets the demands of a global market; and University in the Garden, which fosters shared values, academic leadership, and students who engage in innovative thinking.[19]

In England, JISC worked with the consulting firm CiBIT to develop a scenario planning toolkit. The project identified significant trends, created and tested several scenarios, and produced a final report. Based on two drivers (customer-led vs. institution-driven and inflexible vs. flexible), as shown in figure 9.1, four scenarios were developed and explored. One of these is fictional:[20]

> **Boutique University** (Customer-led/Inflexible). Centered on student learning. Teaching and research are integrated, and the number of disciplines on campus is restricted and focused. The brand of the university dominates life in the university. The Boutique University motto is "Student-focused learning in a secure environment."

More recently, an article suggested that there are four drivers of higher education: the globalization of education, virtualization of education, democratization of education (enhanced student participation), and multiculturalism (new ways of knowing).[21] These scenarios may not, however, be functional in the United States at this time given the importance of institutional and program accreditation, the concern about the affordability of higher education, the desire of some of the nation's governors to cut back funding of higher education severely, and declining budgets that many academic libraries face.

In summary, a review of the scenarios pertaining to the future of higher education is based on a relatively similar set of drivers of change. Among the usual list of suspects are

- New technologies
- Demographics
- Employment necessitating many moves
- Continuing rise in the real cost of education
- Globalization of academic and educational markets
- New competition
- Exponential increase in the growth of knowledge
- The economy

Figure 9.1
JISC (England) Scenario Framework

CUSTOMER-LED

BOUTIQUE UNIVERSITY
(customer-led/inflexible)

- Celebrity status for some, insecurity for most (footballer style deals)
- Very brand conscious
- Narrower range of subjects, probably specialist schools
- Limited info management—concentration on key markets
- Research in specialist areas (attracts status
- Well-defineed
- Standards focus (IT)

MY-U
(customer-led/flexible)

- University of the individual
- Freelancers
- Outsourced course creation & delivery
- Centralised administration (e.g., credit management)
- Standardisation e.g., of libraries
- Lots of information exchange
- Service-driven, quality-led
- High risk
- Research difficult
- Google generation
- Innovation

INFLEXIBLE/STRUCTURED ← → **FLEXIBLE/UNSTRUCTURED**

SCHOLARLY TOWERS
(institution-driven/inflexible)

- Less mobility
- "My way or the highway"
- Clearly defined roles
- Clear hierarchies
- Decentralised
- Known risk
- High self-confidence, strong brand
- Blue skies research easier
- Highly structured
- Dependability
- Long term lock in to IT solutions

MEGA-U
(institution-driven/flexible)

- High volume, high investment (high risk)
- Some permanent staff but lots of consultants too—project-based working
- No need for geographical unity of staff or students
- Strong business cases need making for new courses—do market research
- Commercial drivers for research, product driven
- Respronsive to management
- Core platform (modular)

INSTITUTION-DRIVEN

Source: Reprinted by permission from JISC Netskills, JOS Scenario Planning Project Final Report (2009). © 2009 by HEFCE.

In reviewing a set of scenarios for higher education, which scenario is the most (and least) desirable for a particular situation, and which is the most (and least) likely? The value of such an approach is that it has the potential of stimulating thinking and generating strategies that might not otherwise have been identified.

If a local university has recently developed a new strategic plan, especially if it used scenarios as part of the planning process, the library would be advised to become familiar with all of the associated planning documents that will form the foundation for the library's planning process.

SCENARIOS IN OTHER SETTINGS

Any search engine will reveal sets of scenarios applicable to local government. For instance, one that addresses redevelopment in the city of Buffalo, New York, compares four general scenarios:[22]

Trend, assuming that the City and region continue with planning, capital investment, and development policies and programs similar to those that have been pursued in recent years.

Urban Revitalization, assuming that planning and redevelopment efforts are focused on the revitalization of Buffalo's neighborhoods, house by house and block by block.

Corridor/Activity Center, assuming that redevelopment efforts are directed toward key economic generators such as major transportation corridors and the downtown locale.

Integrated Regional Center, assuming that the City pursues both repair of the urban fabric and redevelopment of key economic generators in an integrated strategy.

Another set of scenarios illustrates "different housing/jobs distribution and transportation infrastructure investments. The scenarios will be evaluated as to how well they help the region to achieve the 15 percent per-capita greenhouse gas emissions reduction target and other . . . performance targets."[23]

Concept of Scenarios Revisited

Rather than attempting to portray accurately (predict) what the future holds, scenarios are constructed around "What if ?" questions about how external forces will affect the organization. We think ahead (plan), considering how alternative future scenarios will play out and determining the degree to which each scenario will likely result in our reaching a particular goal or aspiration. We focus on the community the library serves and the direction the organization needs to go. Associated with each scenario is a degree of risk or uncertainty. Various scenarios are created to explore the ramifications and effects of the uncertainties, as shown in figure 9.2. As time increases, the amount of uncertainty increases.

Figure 9.2
Scenarios Explore the Domain of Uncertainty

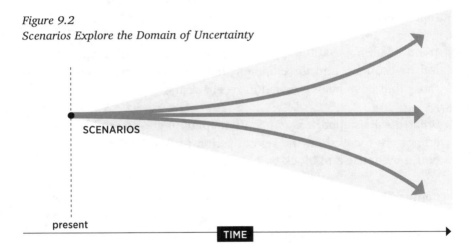

Most scenarios are going to be *wrong* and are never meant to be *right*. The benefits of using scenarios is not a more accurate picture of tomorrow but better thinking about tomorrow by key stakeholders. And this better thinking should challenge the status quo and encourage the library to consider significant changes in the way it delivers its services.

It is not as though the development and use of scenarios are all peaches and cream. Several weaknesses have been noted when an organization attempts to use scenarios in the planning process:

- Scenarios are sometimes crafted by an organization's elites rather than involving a broad cross section of staff members (if not all staff members) to refine and improve each of the scenarios. Everyone who participates in the development of scenarios benefits because they are thinking about the future and what they can do to help their organization be better prepared.
- In some cases, organizational elites arrive at a premature consensus about what the future will look like. To be effective, scenarios must be subject to criticism and revision.
- Some scenarios are fixed at one point in time rather than becoming part of a dynamic process in which they are revisited periodically.

Despite these weaknesses, well-constructed scenarios have immense value and enable libraries to connect with the community served and other stakeholders.

Concluding Thoughts

Lizabeth A. Wilson believes that the most critical question to address is, "Ultimately, how might libraries increase revenue, engender flexibility, foster collaboration, align activities, reduce costs, strengthen infrastructure, and encourage innovation within the framework of a sustainable academic business plan?" She continues,

> We are in the midst of profound change in the way we learn and work. Libraries of all types and sizes have created imaginative spaces that respond to those changes and facilitate learning. Simultaneously, we've been building the Any Time Any Place Library. In doing so, our collective attention has been drawn to how people and libraries interact in a world of ubiquitous, overabundant, and unfiltered digital information. Far from becoming book warehouses, our libraries are vibrant places where people connect and interact with knowledge experts, technology, information, and each other.[24]

The answer to her question must be factored into whatever scenario is preferred and how the organization frames and approaches the future. Still, these are not times to avoid change, embrace the future, and enact substantial change. As Rush Miller points out, "It is not a time for retrenchment and timidity but for expansion and boldness for academic libraries. The library that thrives, even in the midst of a recession, will be the one which seizes the opportunity to redesign itself for the future." He adds,

> I have confidence that even if our vision of the future is imperfect, it is better to be moving forward helping to define the future than to sit back, pat ourselves on the backs for how valuable we always were, and let that future move on without us. We cannot allow anything to deter us from creating the future for libraries that will maintain our relevance to the academic mission of our universities. Even in a recession, we should seize the opportunities it affords us to question our traditions in light of the needs of our users in the digital age. In fact, I say, Damn the Recession, Full Speed Ahead![25]

Miller's advice applies to public libraries and the slow recovery from the recession. In fact, it applies to any time in the present or near future. If he is correct, some libraries will find the scenarios in chapters 5 and 8 too conservative. In such instances, they can be adjusted and made more radical. Still, they represent a foundation from which individual libraries can build as their managerial leaders engage in partnerships; collaborate more broadly (e.g., with nonprofit organizations); develop innovative spaces throughout the building; engage in sustainable thinking; expand the use of digital technology and integrate that technology into the delivery of new services; and, for academic libraries, expand involvement in the curation of information resources. All of these activities require leadership as the organization looks to the future and sees the present as an opportunity for transformational change. However, nothing in this book supports the thesis of Brian T. Sullivan that the academic library, or public library for that matter, will be dead by the year 2050.[26] As different scenario content and actions of a variety of libraries indicate, there are no signs of an "autopsy" report being contemplated.

Libraries will continue to transform and assume new services vital to the communities they serve.

Creativity is the defeat of habit by originality.
—Arthur Koestler

NOTES

1. "The 2012 State of American's Libraries," *American Libraries* (special edition), April 2012, 28, 9, http://americanlibrariesmagazine.org/archives/issue/state-americas-libraries-2012.

2. Richard E. Luce, "A New Value Equation Challenge: The Emergence of eResearch and Roles for Research Libraries" (Washington, DC: Council on Library and Information Resources, 2008), www.clir.org/pubs/reports/pub142/luce.html.

3. For an example, see University of West Florida, Office of the Dean of Libraries, "Institutional Return on Investment (IROI)" (January 2012), http://libguides.uwf.edu/content.php?pid=188487&sid=2184200; and Student Return on Investment (ROI)" (January 2012), http://libguides.uwf.edu/content.php?pid=188487&sid=2183215.

4. For an example, see University of West Florida, Office of the Dean of Libraries, "Calculate Your Personal Return on Investment" (January 2012), http://libguides.uwf.edu/content.php?pid=188487&sid=2261667.

5. See, for instance, Stanley Wilder, *The Age Demographics of Academic Librarians: A Profession Apart* (Binghamton, NY: Haworth Press, 1999).

6. East Carolina University, Joyner Library, job posting: "Instructional Design [Reference] Librarian" (2011), North Carolina Library Association, http://nclaonline.org/forum/job-postings/instructional-design-librarian.

7. For additional examples, see Paula Kaufman, "Let's Get Cozy: Evolving Collaborations in the 21st Century," *Journal of Library Administration* 52, no. 1 (2012): 53–69.

8. Jane Jerrard, Nancy Bolt, and Karen Strege, *Privatizing Libraries* (Chicago: American Library Association, 2012), vii.

9. Scott Bennett, "Designing for Uncertainty: Three Approaches" (2006), 27, 22, 17–18, www.libraryspaceplanning.com/assets/resource/Designing-for-uncertainty_Three-approaches.pdf.

10. Ibid., 20.

11. See Nancy F. Foster and Susan Gibbons, *Studying Students: The Undergraduate Research Project at the University of Rochester* (Chicago: Association of College and Research Libraries, 2007).

12. Maree Conway, "Foresight: Learning from the Future," *Journal of Institutional Research* 12, no. 1 (2002): 1–15. See also Maree Conway, "Scenarios and University Planning," *Journal of Institutional Research* 13, no. 2 (2002): 34–40; Maree Conway and Chris Steward, *Creating and Sustaining Foresight in Australia: A Review of Government Foresight* (Melbourne, Australia: Swinburne University of Technology, Australian Foresight Institute, 2004), http://richardslaughter.com.au/wp-content/uploads/2008/06/AFI_Monograph_08.pdf.

13. James Duderstadt, "A Choice of Transformations for the 21st-Century University," *Chronicle of Higher Education*, February 4, 2000, http://milproj.dc.umich.edu/publications/choice/index.html.

14. Organisation for Economic Co-operation and Development, "The Future of the Tertiary Education Sector: Scenarios for a Learning Society" (Paris: OECD, 2003), http://cals.arizona.edu/dean/planning/six-oecd.pdf.

15. Frank Newman, Lara Couturier, and Jamie Scurry, *The Future of Higher Education: Rhetoric, Reality, and the Risks of the Market* (San Francisco: Jossey-Bass, 2004). As readers review these and other scenarios, they should consider the following recent works: Janna Q. Anderson, Jan L. Boyles, and Lee Rainie, *The Future of Higher Education* (Washington, DC: Pew Research Center's Internet and American Life Project, 2012), http://pewinternet.org/Reports/2012/Future-of-Higher-Education.aspx; Kim Parker, Amanda Lenhart, and Kathleen Moore, *The Digital Revolution and Higher Education* (Washington, DC: Pew Research Center's Internet and American Life Project, 2011), http://pewinternet.org/Reports/2011/College-presidents.aspx; *Study on Research Universities and the Future of America* (Washington, DC: National Research Council, 2012).

16. Stèphan Vincent-Lancrin, "Building Futures Scenarios for Universities and Higher Education: An International Approach," *Policy Futures in Education* 2, no. 2 (Winter 2004): 245–63. See also Paul Lefrere, "Competing Higher Education Futures in a Globalising World," *European Journal of Education* 42, no. 2 (2007): 201–12; Roger L. Caldwell, "Review of Scenarios for Higher Education: Background for Understanding Options for 2010–2015" (2010), http://cals.arizona.edu/dean/planning/January%202010%20Scenarios%20for%202020%20Higher%20Education.pdf; David Collis, "When Industries Change: Scenarios for Higher Education" (1999), http://net.educause.edu/ir/library/pdf/ffp9903.pdf.

17. Organisation for Economic Co-operation and Development, "Four Futures Scenarios for Higher Education," meeting of OECD Education Ministers, June 27–28, 2006, Athens. Reprinted with permission.

18. The University of California Long-Range Guidance Team, *UC 2025: The Power and Promise of Ten* (Berkeley, CA: University of California, 2006), www.universityofcalifornia.edu/future/lrgt1106.pdf. Reprinted with permission.

19. Universiti Sains Malaysia, "Constructing Future Higher Education Scenarios: Insights from Universiti Sains Malaysia" (Pulau Paiang, Malaysia: Universiti Sains Malaysia, 2007), http://globalhighered.files.wordpress.com/2010/08/con_future.pdf.

20. JISC, *JOS Scenario Planning Project—Final Report* (July 2009), www.jisc.ac.uk/media/documents/programmes/jos/jos%20scenario%20planning%20project%20final%20report.pdf. See also JISC's "Our Libraries of the Future Campaign," www.jisc.ac.uk/whatwedo/campaigns/librariesofthefuture.aspx; and others recent research programs as www.jisc.ac.uk/whatwedo/.

21. Sohail Inayatullah, "University Futures: Wikipedia Uni, Core-Periphery Reversed, Incremental Managerialism or Bliss for All?" *On the Horizon* 20, no. 1 (2012): 84–91.

22. City of Buffalo (New York) Comprehensive Plan, "2.2 Development Scenarios," www.ci.buffalo.ny.us/files/1_2_1/Mayor/COB_Comprehensive_Plan/section_24595526187.html.

23. One Bay Area, "Plan Bay Area: Planning Scenarios" (2011), www.onebayarea.org/plan_bay_area/land_use.htm.

24. Lizabeth A. Wilson, "Creating Sustainable Futures for Academic Libraries," *Journal of Library Administration* 52, no. 1 (2012): 78–93, http://dx.doi.org/10.1080/01930826.2012.630241.

25. Rush Miller, "Damn the Recession, Full Speed Ahead," *Journal of Library Administration* 52, no. 1 (2012): 3–17, http://dx.doi.org/10.1080/01930826.2012.629963.

26. Brian T. Sullivan, "Academic Library Autopsy Report, 2050," *Chronicle of Higher Education*, January 2, 2011, http://chronicle.com/article/article-content/125767/.

APPENDIX A

The Use of Scenarios in the Pierce County Library System

NEEL PARIKH

Pierce County Library System (PCLS), the fourth largest library system in the state of Washington, serves 555,000 people over 1,800 square miles through eighteen library branches. The library system is an independent taxing district serving suburban communities with pockets of rural and remote populations. The library recently used scenarios in two different situations, both in conjunction with facilities planning.

LIBRARY ENVISIONING THE FUTURE

In fall 2008, prior to beginning a facilities master-planning process, the library's Executive Team used scenarios to help envision alternative futures for the library. Consultants Joan Frye Williams and George Needham, after evaluating the overall library system, challenged the team to examine eight strategic questions. The questions described a trend and asked what county residents would expect from the library and how the library would respond. The point of the exercise was to begin to lay the groundwork for the future of the PCLS.

In the beginning, the exercise was challenging. The Executive Team grappled with differentiating between answering the question from the perspective of the resident and answering how the library would respond. We were challenged to look at each trend from the customers' perspective and imagine their expectations. To jump-start the conversation, we took the following example for mobile computing:

> More and more, Pierce County residents are using cell phones, iPhones, Blackberries and other personal devices for communicating with service providers and each other. In the future, what results do you think residents will expect from their library in light of this trend?

We envisioned a variety of possibilities, such as that residents would

- Have the same experience they have now—no change.
- Have the same experience with PCLS that they would have with any good library—so PCLS will identify and follow the prevailing professional library practice.
- Have the same experience with PCLS that they have with other local service providers—so PCLS will identify and follow the prevailing local practice.
- Communicate with PCLS using the highest possible quality mobile technology, that is, customers will choose and use the best one to communicate with PCLS using whatever mainstream technology is most convenient for them—so PCLS will offer multiple communication options and residents will opt in based on individual preference.

Given these options, it was easier to develop an answer applicable to our situation. We chose the last option. That answer formed the final proposal. The next question was tied to growth in eastern Pierce County:

> The Eastern portion of Pierce County is the fastest growing part of the PCLS service area so demand for services is likely to increase. In the future, what results do you think residents will expect from their library in the light of this trend?

Our first attempt at a response was inadequate, and so we were challenged to look at the question more deeply—to think of ourselves as residents living in a suburban area, distant from services, and commuting over an hour every day. We were also challenged to explain when we would build a library and what services would we offer. Our resulting scenario was

> Growth in Pierce County: In the future, what results will residents expect from their library in light of eastern Pierce County being the fastest growing part of the Library's service area?
>
> Residents expect to have a library near them and convenient, and that provides services equal to what they think others receive. So, Pierce County Library System will pay attention to the development and growth of eastern Pierce County, and it will offer and provide multiple options to deliver services as communities grow.
>
> The Library will regularly/annually review population changes and growth in regions throughout the Library's service area and determine how to serve growing communities.
>
> As growth occurs, the Library will offer and provide various options to serve growing communities, such as book drops, kiosks, mailing materials, and bookmobile service. In 2009, the Library's Community Outreach Services Department will examine services in areas including regions previously identified as rural and remote. That examination will include establishing criteria for offering outreach services such as book drops and kiosks.
>
> The Library will build larger buildings and fewer smaller buildings, with 10,000 to 15,000 square feet being a minimum size. The library will develop "community spaces" in addition to book and learning spaces. The Library will use the following criteria to determine building a branch in a new area. It will review the area to determine if it has a majority of the following elements:
>
> • Isolated geographically
> • Existing and projected population of 20,000 or more and population density

- Expenditure equity across the district
- Transportation corridors
- Identified community
- The presence of some commercial infrastructure, such as shopping, post office, and banking.

Because of the thought involved in creating this document, the Executive Team really understood and acknowledged what the conditions would be for the customer and what the possible ramifications were for the library system.

A later question examined "Front Line Customer Engagement":

> PCLS emphasizes customer focused service throughout its mission, vision and values statements and has identified specific behaviors for how front line staff should engage library customers. These behaviors emphasize greeting customers and empathizing with them. At the same time, self-directed self options such as self checkout and customer placed holds are increasing, and Pierce County residents are generally free to choose how and when they will engage with the library staff. In future, what results do you think customers will expect from their library in light of this trend?

At this point our responses to these questions were more in-depth and examined in great detail the range of customer needs. Besides examining levels of service and expectations, one comment in the library's response stated, "Staff's primary job is to be available and approachable for all residents and to recognize those who need assistance and be pro-active about offering it."

We also explored topics such as "the changing nature of reading," "collections—mass market or long tail," "demographic changes," "scarcity versus abundance," "teen services," and "energy costs." It is interesting that, although these trends were presented to us in 2008, with some adjustment they still hold true today.

Results

The growth scenario became the standard for the work of the Facilities Master Plan. The plan followed the recommendation of having large buildings and fewer small buildings, making 10,000 square feet the minimum size. It also included the recommendation for alternative service delivery units located in areas easily accessible to a highly mobile population. This concept became embedded in our practice such that, when communities (such as a new housing development) came to us to discuss library service, we were ready to offer kiosks as an interim measure to provide convenient service before building a full-size branch. In 2010 the library began extensive reevaluation of its bookmobile service within the context of this scenario. Bookmobile stops to rural communities were eliminated; one two-hour visit every two weeks to a small community was not seen as effective. This was the first step in a change in the direction of service, seeking to serve these isolated communities more effectively through online service or alternative service delivery units in the future.

The "Front Line Customer Engagement" scenario became the basis for a serious discussion about how to deliver customer service in the future. The Facilities Master Plan envisioned a single desk in branches. As we grappled with how service would be delivered from a single desk, we worked again with consultants Williams and Needham and developed a service model called "The Experience Model." Many elements of the customer engagement scenario were incorporated in 2009 budget cuts when staffing was restructured to match this different pattern of service.

We also used the scenario technique with the top-level library managers. The intent was to help them look at the future from the customers' perspective. It was a valuable exercise. New ideas came to the surface. We did discover that the librarians on the team tended to describe how the library would respond and the nonlibrarians on the team were more effective at envisioning the future from the customers' perspective.

COMMUNITY ENVISIONING THE FUTURE

In February 2009 the library system hosted a community strategic visioning workshop, "Building Value in Our Communities." Fifty-seven community leaders gathered for a full-day workshop to speculate on how PCLS would align its services and facilities with the community's vision of life in 2030. The workshop was part of an ongoing collaboration with community leaders to develop a vision for PCLS rooted firmly in community needs and priorities. It was one of several public involvement opportunities in the facilities master planning process.

The master plan consultants, Group 4 Architecture, Research + Planning, facilitated the all-day workshop, which led the group through a series of focused activities to develop ideas about the future, using visioning techniques to encourage visionary thinking and discussions. Participants compared the library to other community symbols and images and used the attribute of other destinations, brands, and services to identify what residents wanted from their library. From this exercise emerged a series of vision statements that the library explored as a part of its planning process.

Participants were given symbols, such as farmers' market, iPhone, Mt. Rainier, and asked to record the most distinguishing characteristics and qualities of the symbol. They were then asked to consider how the qualities and characteristics of this symbol could be used as a metaphor for defining a hypothetical library. Finally, small groups joined together to create their hypothetical library. The imagination and creativity of the community members were amazing. The community had a huge vision for the library, drawing a picture with words of a library central to community life. Their pictures were woven into stories for the workshop report. Here are two examples:

> **The Bridge Library** combines the best attributes of a place such as Facebook, a service such as a farmers' market, and the values of the public schools. This library has the ability to connect everyone. It embraces technology, but at the same time it recognizes the value of people as individuals with a need to stay connected both in person and online. This library supports the community. It is a comprehensive, affordable, and happening place. It emphasizes retaining history while offering something for everyone at every stage of life.

> **Home with a View Library** combines the best attributes of a place such as Mt. Rainier, services such as Google, and the values of the Forza Coffee Company (a local coffee company with living room–type amenities). In this perspective, the library is beautiful and strong. It is a destination structure and an icon, a

treasure of the community. This library is both historically significant and sustainable to last the test of generations. Services include leading technology, with customized databases. The library is a gathering place where people enjoy their coffee in a comfortable, welcoming atmosphere.

These stories were not just powerful and uplifting; they also expanded our imagination for what the future library could be. The most interesting result was that this story-like quality resonated well with staff—much better than the language of a strategic plan. The staff grabbed onto the stories as our future strategic plan for the library. Throughout the next few years, people would quote the stories or use them as an image for future services.

Results

The immediate result was that the community members who participated were very excited about the process and were glad to have been engaged and involved. An architect who had participated in the workshop commented to me that he was experienced in providing this kind of visioning, but this was the best one he had ever seen. It seemed that the conversation helped participants not only see a bigger role for the library but also think about their relationship with the library in a very different manner. Over the past few years, participants in that workshop have contacted us and suggested many different ways the library might collaborate with their organization or in the community. It definitely helped expand their vision of the role for the library.

Another result was staff interest in exploring new approaches. Not only have we engaged in new partnerships, but library staff are creating innovative ways to reach into and support the community. This includes everything from partnering with a food bank to collect food for military families, to partnering with local unemployment services to deliver job search training, to creating online (via the website) a teen summer reading program as a game with badges. A local literacy program approached us recently seeking the library as a grant partner to assist people to meet the requirements for U.S. citizenship. This was recognition of the role of the library as a community site and a place to draw people who would not travel into an urban setting.

CONCLUSION

It is clear that scenarios engage management and staff in speculation and lead to an exploration of new ideas. Because a scenario is not a plan that needs to be implemented, it allows one to dream. The dreaming can be scary because it could suggest expensive, new, or unusual options. But allowing us to dream big was the first step toward actually changing and doing new, big, different things.

ACKNOWLEDGMENTS

Joan Frye Williams, consultant; George Needham, consultant; David Schnee, Dawn Merkes, and Kari Svanstrom, Group 4 Architecture, Research + Planning, Inc. (South San Francisco).

APPENDIX B

The Anythink Revolution

PAM SANDLIAN-SMITH

S tarting a revolution requires courage, tenacity, passion, and a whole lot of creativity. It requires strong leadership, an environment that welcomes ideas, and a team of people with the drive and determination to reach for the stars. This was the formula for success at Anythink Libraries in Adams County, Colorado. Once the worst-funded library district in the state as it entered a new century, the suburban library district just north of Denver made a radical transformation to one of the most innovative library systems in the country.

SHOOT FOR THE MOON

In November 2006, residents of Adams County approved a mill levy increase that essentially tripled Rangeview Library District's operating budget. With this new funding in hand, the district board of trustees knew they had to be strategic about how they invested taxpayers' funds. They wanted to build libraries for the future—not just for the present.

They also understood that to do this required visionary leadership. I was selected for the job. As former head of the children's library at Denver Public Library and, more recently, the director of West Palm Beach (Fla.) Public Library, I have a "shoot for the moon" attitude and I am passionate about creating spaces for people.

"Shoot for the moon" is a phrase that a good friend of mine used often when I worked at the Denver Public Library when we were building the new Central Library, which opened in 1995. When we were designing that space, we gave it our all, working with the architects to create a space that supported children and their myriad needs. Understanding how libraries and librarians need to listen and observe their customers as well as be cognizant of their competition has always been important to me.

When I interviewed for this position, I told the interview team not to hire me if they wanted to have a regular, vanilla library. My job as a leader is to challenge assumptions and to raise the bar high, to encourage us to "shoot for the moon" in bringing about our best efforts to design, implement, and operate a thriving library for the twenty-first century.

A UNIFIED VISION

Though strong leadership is key, one person can do only so much. The most important thing a leader can do is surround herself with driven, innovative team members with a cohesive vision. Before I even started the job at Anythink, I had a good sense that there was synergy with the team already in place. The management team was light-hearted, progressive, and tight knit.

Inspired by a West Palm Beach vision project, the library management team encouraged all staff to submit words that described the type of library they wanted to be. Right off, we imagined a library that was majestic, soaring, welcoming, and inspiring. We all read Jim Collins's *Good to Great and the Social Sectors* (HarperCollins, 2005) and did the diagnostics. That was pretty tough and very revealing. We began working on scenarios, though we called them models. We examined product, relationship, and value models and then turned to our own invention, which we called an experience model. The board decided that the experience model was the direction it wanted the district to go. This influenced the direction of the 2008–2010 strategic plan.

The team began working on essential projects, including design development for the new libraries, weeding, community analysis, development of the district's customer service philosophy, and branding. The team bonded as the members worked together and, in many cases, invented strategy on the fly. A couple of key elements kept us coming back to the center: designing our libraries and services for our customers, and finding ways to make the user experience delightful, comfortable, and intuitive.

With all the changes that were happening at the district, it was important to build on the energy and philosophies being developed and to hire people who were in line with those philosophies. The organization was looking for a combination of skills and competencies. Before we even defined the competencies, we were looking for people who were creative, innovative, problem solvers, collaborators, and had a high degree of emotional intelligence and maturity.

ANYTHINK INVENTS US

One of the challenges of changing so drastically, so quickly, is ensuring that staff are on board. Of course, in Rangeview Library District's case they had been the underdogs for so long that there was nowhere to go but up. With that said, the Anythink team used several different strategies to build its culture and give staff the sense that they were a part of something bigger than themselves.

One key element that cannot be overlooked: The library district personnel as a whole had aspirations to become a world-class library. I could not have made one change if this characteristic had not been evident from the beginning. Though our efforts have evolved, many elements remain the same. We had a silo effect in our branches, and we needed to put teams together to work on problems collaboratively. We formed task groups to work on issues like customer service and growing the culture. We included staff at all different levels—shelvers, clerical, librarians, managers, and administration. These teams solved some of our core issues. Our customer service team drafted our initial customer service document, which turned into our "13 Brilliant Steps to Customer Service." They suggested that we eliminate fines, and we took this to the library board.

Another of our task groups, led by Anythink human resources director Susan Dobbs, is responsible for growing and sustaining a culture of optimism at the organization. Called the Yellow Geckos, they developed wellness programs, hikes, snowshoeing adventures, karaoke night, and Anythink's annual bowling night, the most anticipated staff event of the year.

People form teams of five and come up with silly team names like The Bowling Stones; Eat, Pray, Bowl; and The Bowling Lebowskis—they even dress up in costumes and talk smack for weeks beforehand. It is such a silly thing, but it works on so many levels.

Barn raising is a metaphor frequently used to describe how Anythink accomplished some of its biggest tasks, including weeding, RFID, opening new buildings, and remapping the collection from the Dewey Decimal System to WordThink, Anythink's word-based classification. We have created a culture where everyone chips in, and we have created bonds throughout the district in this way.

Anythink has adopted the FISH philosophy and trainings, inspired by Seattle's Pikes Place Fish Market, as tools to continue to grow the organization's culture. The FISH philosophy includes four simple, interconnected practices:

> **Be There** is being emotionally present for people. It is a powerful message of respect that improves communication and strengthens relationships.

> **Play** taps into your natural way of being creative, enthusiastic, and having fun. Play is the spirit that drives the curious mind, as in "Let's play with that idea." It is a mindset you can bring to everything you do.

> **Make Their Day** is finding simple ways to serve or delight people in a meaningful, memorable way. It is about contributing to someone else's life, not because you want something out of it, but because that is the person you want to be.

Choose Your Attitude means taking responsibility for how you respond to what life throws at you. Once you are aware that your choice impacts everyone around you, you can ask yourself, "Is my attitude helping my team or my customers? Is it helping me to be the person I want to be?"

One thing that works for us is that we are not afraid to try things. Some things go over like a lead balloon. Some things work, and those are the things that stick. Our story has become one that is very inspirational and fun for us all to tell, so our own urban legend of how we turned the organization around helps support and maintain our culture. Because so many of the changes that were made at Anythink required a team effort, pride of ownership has emerged among staff.

From the beginning, Anythink leadership engaged staff at all levels in the visioning process. This continues today, as when all staff contributed to the development of the district's 2012–2014 strategic plan. We have also had our fair share of negativity and naysayers. We thoughtfully addressed this and let it be known that that attitude did not really belong in this organization. So we tried to be honest with each other when things were not working, and slowly but surely our culture evolved into a supportive, fun, positive environment. In short, we have reoriented the way we think about our work. Recently, one of our staff members said, "People say we invented Anythink, but Anythink invents us. It has completed changed the way I think about my work, even my family. I have become a different person. I have learned to live with ambiguity."

EXPERIENCE SOMETHING DIFFERENT

Part of creating a new culture at Anythink was changing the way staff do their work at the library. The type of work they do has changed significantly from the tasks they had five years ago. During the peak of the district's reinvention, new job roles were created and all frontline staff were asked to reapply for their positions, with the caveat that no one would lose their jobs and no one would lose their pay.

The previous job descriptions used by the district were between ten and fifteen years old and were originally implemented through the Adams County human resources department. They were outdated and no longer reflected the work being done at the libraries. Also, there were many levels, like library assistant I, II, III, but the distinctions between these levels were not clear. As often happens, when something is undefined it opens the door for people to fill in the gaps and to invent their own definitions—in this case job descriptions. Between branches, there was significant disparity in what one person might do under the same job title.

When I was in West Palm, we had worked with Ritz Carlton on hospitality and customer service. One of their key messages was that they always hired for a few key competencies, including work ethic, people orientation, and job ownership. I had been working on creating competency-based job descriptions there as well.

Much clarification was needed, especially with the new service philosophy and new workflows with things like WordThink being implemented. The Anythink administrative team spent hours listing all of the skills, jobs, and so forth that were needed day to day to run the branches. These were placed into "buckets," which turned out to be the materials-handling bucket, the hospitality bucket, and the planner-professional bucket. These became what Anythink now calls wranglers, concierges, and guides. Anythink's job descriptions are now synced with the passion and vision of the district. All of the district's job roles are based on key competencies that connect to Anythink's customer service philosophy.

DESIGN FOR PEOPLE

The drastic changes in service philosophy—and branding—also influenced the design of Anythink's new buildings. Over the course of three years, the district built four new libraries and renovated three existing libraries. It was important for the district leadership to strive for that "unique emotional space" when people walked into the new buildings.

Because some of the design planning had started prior to my joining the team, some reconfiguring had to occur. Architect Dennis Humphries and his team had been working on plans; in a couple of cases, they were finished with design development. After reviewing the plans carefully, I asked that we start from scratch and that the only way I knew to be successful was to take all of the books out of the plans and begin anew. Thank goodness Dennis and his team were willing to rethink the projects. In some cases they had to start over completely, but in the end the decisions made everything work out so much better.

The words provided by staff in the original visioning process were used as inspiration for the buildings' designs. Our libraries needed to be majestic, soaring, natural, whimsical, playful, and inspiring, to name a few. Our spaces needed to be flexible and accommodate the way people use our spaces. These included

- Noisy collaboration
- Quite collaboration
- Media experiences—gaming/movies
- Comfortable seating for individuals and for groups
- Quiet study space
- Popular materials and display, designed for impulse purchases
- Activity area for messy work in the children's spaces
- Active area
- Craft space
- Space for preschool-toddler-baby-families
- Iconic space (tree houses!)
- Bookstore organization
- Convenient, fast pickup and checkout
- Computers and computer labs
- Program/learning spaces
- Book club space
- Flexibility

As a team we had to keep coming back to these concepts and criteria. Designing libraries for people and how they use space is a different process than focusing on space planning involving contents of the library, including books, tables, and chairs, and making projections for increased space needs as collections grow and usage patterns change. Anythink's design team worked with the interior designers to develop spaces where the bookshelves formed smaller rooms instead of the traditional rows of book shelving typically found in libraries. There is a huge emphasis on flexibility and openness that is apparent in all of

Anythink's libraries. Thank goodness we were able to start fresh. We made our book shelving fit around these activities. Now we have amazing flexibility because we can remake our spaces fairly easily by simply rearranging shelving for the most part.

THE FLAG WE MARCH BEHIND

Over the course of my library career, I have come to realize the importance of marketing, branding, and image. In West Palm Beach, I learned a lot from working with design consultant Peter Robinson on the importance of a cohesive look, brand, presentation, style, and so forth. With all of the changes happening, the district needed a new image that better reflected the type of library it was becoming. Rangeview Library District also had a bit of an identity crisis. For so long, community members were used to driving past their libraries to others in Westminster, Denver, or Broomfield. Over 70 percent of the population in Adams County is fifty years of age or younger, and district leadership understood that they needed a brand that could compete with the likes of Google, Barnes and Noble, and Starbucks.

How we look, how we present ourselves as a library, all of our publications, need to promote the brand, the image of the library, in a consistent manner. Each interaction with a touch point creates an opportunity to imprint a relationship with the product or service. When we were testing the new brand with marketing students, they told us, "In my mind libraries are dead. I never go to a library, but if you introduce this kind of brand, I would give you another chance, I would try it out. . . . You have to do something dramatic to compete."

The marketing concept of features, benefits, and emotional space consistently influences many of the decisions made at Anythink. The first tier of the concept concentrates on features. Many libraries market features when they talk about programs, materials, computers, databases, and the like. The next tier is about benefits, which is more powerful. Library benefits include learning how to read, spending time with friends or family, getting to know your community, learning a new skill that enriches or enhances your life, and creating something that has an impact on your life.

The most powerful marketing tier is creating a unique emotional space and connection that your brand owns. Apple and Nike are two brands that create that unique emotional connection. We want Anything to be the brand people have a unique emotional connection to. It is beginning to happen. It definitely has happened with the staff. Anything has become a way of life, a way of thinking about work, about engaging with our community, about inventing a different kind of library that is a partner in the success of our community and our customers.

Our board of directors took a big risk in agreeing to work on this project; they were part of the RFP process and selection of the marketing firm that we worked with to create Anythink. The board took an even bigger risk in adapting Anythink and the doodle as our new brand. As we were reviewing our successes over the past years, one board member commented on the brand: "I am so glad that we got it right. I wasn't sure when we were having all of those discussions about the brand, but we made the right decision. Recently, my mom died of Alzheimer's. She could not remember me or my dad, but when my dad would be driving her past one of the libraries, she would see the big Anythink sign and point and say, 'Anythink, that's Linda's library.'"

ABOUT THE AUTHORS

Peter Hernon is a professor at Simmons College, Graduate School of Library and Information Science, Boston, and the principal faculty member for the doctoral program Managerial Leadership in the Information Professions. He received his PhD degree from Indiana University, Bloomington, is the 2008 recipient of the ACRL's Academic/Research Librarian of the Year award, is the coeditor of *Library & Information Science Research*, and has taught, conducted workshops, and delivered addresses internationally. He is the author or coauthor of fifty-two books, including *Assessing Service Quality* (American Library Association, 1998, 2010) and *Viewing Library Metrics from Different Perspectives* (Libraries Unlimited, 2009).

Joseph R. Matthews is a consultant specializing in strategic planning, assessment, evaluation of library services, customer service, use of performance measures, and the balanced scorecard. He was an instructor at the San Jose State University School of Library and Information Science. He is author of *The Customer-Focused Library* (Libraries Unlimited, 2009), *The Evaluation and Measurement of Library Services* (Libraries Unlimited, 2007), *Scorecards for Results* (Libraries Unlimited, 2008), *Strategic Planning and Management for Managers* (Libraries Unlimited, 2005), and *Measuring for Results* (Libraries Unlimited, 2003) and the coauthor (with Peter Hernon) of *Listening to the Customer* (Libraries Unlimited, 2011), among other books.

Robert E. Dugan the dean of libraries, University of West Florida (Pensacola). Prior to assuming this position, he had been at Suffolk University in Boston; Wesley College in Dover, Delaware; and Georgetown University in Washington, D.C. He has also worked in state and public libraries during his nearly forty-year career.

Richard Fyffe has been librarian at Grinnell College, Iowa, since 2006. From 2000 to 2006 he was assistant dean of libraries for scholarly communication at the University of Kansas, Lawrence, where he oversaw collection development, policy for electronic licensing, and preservation and co-led the digital initiatives program, including development of the digital repository KU ScholarWorks. He has written articles and made presentations in areas related to scholarly communication, information policy, and digital preservation and served on the ACRL Scholarly Communications Committee, the *College and Research Libraries* editorial board, the board of directors for the Center for Research Libraries, and the board of directors for *BioOne*.

Diane J. Graves is university librarian and professor at Trinity University, San Antonio, a position she has held since 2001. In that role, she focuses on information literacy, marketing services to students and faculty, and promoting positive change from the traditional academic library to a more dynamic service and access environment. Graves is active in EDUCAUSE and the Oberlin Group of Library Directors and served as an elected member of the SPARC Steering Committee. She was selected by the ACRL as the recipient of the 2007 Excellence in Academic Libraries Award, College Division.

Danuta A. Nitecki has provided programmatic oversight for several academic library renovation and building projects over the past three decades. At Drexel University, where she has been dean of libraries since 2010, she helped introduce the concept of the library as an embedded learning environment and is currently engaging stakeholders in envisioning a renovated W. W. Hagerty Library. Serving as an associate university librarian at Yale University Library (1996–2010), she had administrative responsibilities for public services, including managing the design and implementation of an off-site shelving facility and a complete library renovation. Nitecki has been active in national, state, and regional associations; has served as a consultant; and has written over fifty articles, books, and compilations on such topics as library spaces, user-based evaluation of library services, research methods, document delivery, and management of library services and information technology applications.

Neel Parikh is executive director of the Pierce County Library System, Tacoma, Washington. Prior to this, she served as chief of branch libraries and coordinator of children's services for the San Francisco Public Library. She is active in national professional associations and has served as president of the California Library Association, member of the board of the Public Library Association, and chair of the Urban Youth Strategy Group and Capacity Building Strategy Group of the Urban Libraries Council. She is currently the chair of the Early Learning Public Library Partnership in Washington State. Under her leadership, the Pierce County Library System was awarded a 2011 Urban Libraries Council Innovation Award. Parikh is a fellow of the American Leadership Forum and serves on its local board of directors. In 2012 she was honored by the *Business Examiner* as an outstanding female leader in the South Puget Sound, receiving a "Woman of Influence, Lifetime Achievement" award.

Pam Sandlian-Smith, director of Anythink Libraries in Thornton, Colorado, was previously the director of the West Palm Beach (Florida) Public Library and the children's services manager at the Denver Public Library. She is the recipient of the 2012 Charlie Robinson Award for risk taking and innovation in public libraries. Anythink has been awarded the 2010 National Medal for Museum and Library Service and the 2011 John Cotton Dana Public Relations Award and was a 2011 Library Journal Landmark Library.

INDEX

Locators in *italic* refer to figures/diagrams